ROUTLEDGE LIBRARY EDITIONS:
RESPONDING TO FASCISM

HITLER'S OFFICIAL PROGRAMME

HITLER'S OFFICIAL PROGRAMME
And Its Fundamental Ideas

GOTTFRIED FEDER

Volume 1

Routledge
Taylor & Francis Group

LONDON AND NEW YORK

First published in English 1934

This edition first published in 2010
by Routledge
2 Park Square, Milton Park, Abingdon, Oxon, OX14 4RN

Simultaneously published in the USA and Canada
by Routledge
711 Third Avenue, New York, NY 10017

Routledge is an imprint of the Taylor & Francis Group, an informa business

First issued in paperback 2013

British Library Cataloguing in Publication Data
A catalogue record for this book is available from the British Library

ISBN 13: 978-0-415-57699-4 (Set)
eISBN 13: 978-0-203-85012-1 (Set)
ISBN 13: 978-0-415-58081-6 (Volume 1)
ISBN 13: 978-0-415-84885-5 (Volume 1)
eISBN 13: 978-0-203-85024-4 (Volume 1)

Publisher's Note
The publisher has gone to great lengths to ensure the quality of this reprint but
points out that some imperfections in the original copies may be apparent.

Disclaimer
The publisher has made every effort to trace copyright holders and would
welcome correspondence from those they have been unable to trace.

HITLER'S

Official Programme

and its Fundamental Ideas

LONDON
George Allen & Unwin Ltd
MUSEUM STREET

Published in Germany by Frz. Eher Nachf. G.m.b.H., Munich, the official publishers to the National Socialist Party (Zentralverlag der N.S.D.A.P.)

THIS TRANSLATION FIRST PUBLISHED 1934

RE-ISSUED 1938

The Publisher's Note is dated 1934

PUBLISHER'S NOTE

The engineer Gottfried Feder, now a Secretary of State, was asked by Adolf Hitler to formulate the official Programme of the German National Socialist Party. This was first published in August 1927 under the title *Das Programm der N.S.D.A.P.* The present book is a full and faithful translation of the fifth German edition of this book, printed in 1934 and then in its seven hundred and seventy-fifth thousand.

The Twenty-five Points announced on February 25, 1920, from the Hofbräu Brewery, Munich, are included in the original and in the translation.

PREFACE[1]

At Weimar, in 1926, the Council of the Party decided to publish a series of pamphlets which should deal in a concise form with fundamental questions affecting every aspect of political life in Germany. Our intention was, and is, to present a complete and consistent picture of the attitude of National Socialism toward the various tasks of our public life, and of the means by which it hopes to remove its errors and defects.

Our task is therefore to examine exhaustively *its present state*, *its origin*, and finally to give a constructive answer to the fateful question, *what next*? The principal aim of these pamphlets is to indicate new modes of political life, of finance, and of economics; consequently these works should and must differ from essays of the sort usually published, which are so "scientific" that they dare not go beyond the retrospective surveys of the "historians," and so "objective" and "matter-of-fact" that they dare not express any definite opinion. The object of this series of pamphlets is to set up *un rocher de bronze* in the midst of chaos, by exhaustive study to arrive at clear knowledge, and to shape, in the light of this knowledge, a united political will.

[1] Containing the gist of the prefaces to the first, fourth, and fifth German editions, and the preface to the 326th–350th thousand.

At the great meeting on August 31, 1927, Adolf Hitler declared emphatically: "Questions of Programme do not concern the Council of Administration; the Programme is fixed, and I shall never suffer changes in the principles of the movement as laid down in its Programme." With this decisive pronouncement on the part of our Leader I associate myself whole-heartedly, for nothing is more dangerous to the existence and the striking force of a movement such as ours than the subjection of its principles to negative criticism and discussion.

No man who feels that he cannot go the whole way with us in the Jewish question, in our fight against high finance, the Dawes Pact, and the pauperizing policy of our opponents, or in any other questions contained in our Programme, or who is inclined, in a spirit of compromise and cowardice, to barter the liberty of the German nation through the League of Nations or the Locarno Pact, need apply to us; his place is outside the N.S.D.A.P. We utterly reject the "superior" private opinions which such persons are so ready to air in their platform oratory and journalistic out-pourings.

A man who agrees fundamentally with our principles may perhaps have scruples about a few minor details, for we cannot expect everyone to agree absolutely on all questions, especially in an aggressive political movement. It is, however, a different matter when outsiders or political enemies attack some particular point by odious misrepresentations. In such a case an official commentary is necessary (see pp. 40–41, Point 17).

We refuse to vary our Programme for reasons of expediency, as other Parties do, to suit so-called altered conditions. We intend to make conditions suit our Programme, by mastering them.

I have been commissioned by Adolf Hitler to issue this series of pamphlets, which are to form the official literature of the Party.

During the electoral campaign for the Presidency of the Reich the 326th–350th thousands of our "Programme" have been published, in order to proclaim the ideas and the objects of the National Socialists.

While bewilderment, anxiety and chaos prevail in the bourgeois camp, while the Governmental Marxists are making ridiculous and convulsive attempts at suppression, the N.S.D.A.P. is following an upward course at a rate unprecedented in Party history, and preparing to achieve political power.

Our Programme, our aims, are unaltered. No essential corrections of any kind have been made, and none are necessary.

We refuse to do as other Parties do—to adapt our Programme, on grounds of expediency, to the so-called circumstances. We shall simply adapt the circumstances to our Party, by making ourselves the masters of circumstances.

The following official Party Manifesto of March 6, 1930, has been included, and also my rejoinder to the questions which the leading organ of the Reichslandbund, the *Deutsche Tageszeitung*, addressed to us; which rejoinder was likewise inserted in that journal.

This is the best and most forcible refutation of all the lies concerning our alleged hostile attitude to *German agriculture* in respect of *property and the right of inheritance*.

CONTENTS

INTRODUCTION

HISTORICAL ACCOUNT OF THE RISE OF THE N.S.D.A.P.
WITH A BIOGRAPHICAL SURVEY OF THE CAREER
OF ADOLF HITLER[1]

Adolf Hitler was born on April 20, 1889, at Braunau
on the Inn, a village of the old Bavaria.

His father, the son of a poor peasant, worked his
way up to the post of Customs official. His mother
came of a German peasant family. When he was
thirteen years of age he lost his father, and four years
later his mother. Adolf Hitler was then a pupil at the
Realschule at Linz on the Danube, having previously
passed through the National School. It had been his
father's wish that he should become an official, but
his own ambition was to become an artist. His mother's
death obliged him without further delay to earn his
own living.

At seventeen years of age Hitler went to Vienna,
where he aimed at becoming an architect. He earned
a living by his own efforts, first as a builder's labourer,
than as an architectural draughtsman. Already he
was beginning to take an interest in politics; he
became an anti-Marxist, but so far he played no

[1] This introduction does not appear in the German
edition, but in an English translation issued by the
Zentralverlag der N.S.D.A.P., the last section having been
revised for the English edition by the Zentralverlag, in
order to bring it up to date.

active part in political life. From his earliest youth Hitler had been a passionate Nationalist, and his hope was to combine the social experiences of his working period with his nationalist convictions. For several years he lived in Vienna in extreme poverty.

In 1912 he migrated to Munich, where he lived the life of a student. He had never known anything of the pleasures and amusements natural to youth; but ever since the day when he left home with fifty kronen in his pocket labour and privation had been his lot.

In February 1914 he succeeded in getting free of the obligation to serve in the Austrian Army. Six months later war broke out. He immediately volunteered for service in the German Army, and obtained, by a direct appeal to King Ludwig of Bavaria, permission to enter a Bavarian regiment as a volunteer for the duration of the war. On October 10, 1914, the new regiment marched forth.

On December 2, 1914, Hitler was awarded the Iron Cross of the second class.

In recognition of his bravery in the attack on the "Bayernwald" and in other engagements near Wytschaete, he was ordered to serve as despatch-bearer, a duty which called for especial courage and reliability, as reports had often to be carried across open ground under heavy fire. This quickly made his name known throughout the regiment, beyond the narrow circle of his comrades.

On October 7, 1916, he was wounded by a shell-splinter. In March 1917 he returned to his regiment. He received several other distinctions, including a *Regiments-Diplom* for special bravery in the fighting near Fontaines, and finally the Iron Cross of the first class.

On October 14, 1918, he was severely injured, along with many of his regimental comrades, by the mustard-gas which the British were then using for the first time, and he was temporarily blinded. While he was in hospital the Revolution broke out.

On this Hitler resolved to become a politician. In 1919 he joined a small party consisting of six members, and with them he founded the National Socialist German Workers' Party. He drew up in outline the Programme of the new movement, and settled its character and aims.

THE NUCLEUS: SEVEN MEN

In September 1919 Adolf Hitler made his first speech to seven men; he then addressed audiences of 11, 25, 47; in December, of 111; in January 1920 of 270, and shortly afterwards of 400. On November 14, 1920, he spoke at a mass meeting of 1,700. He now organized the propaganda of the young Party, which after a year's work numbered 64 members. A year later—1921—it already numbered 3,000. Hitler's propagandist activity in Munich was such that he was finally addressing mass meetings three times a week, and on Mondays he carried on a course of instruction. He attacked first and foremost the *folly of Versailles,*

B

and denied the assertions of the Marxists, the Centre
Party, etc., that it was possible to fulfil the Treaty.
He pilloried the slogan of these Parties: "Give up
your arms, and the others also will disarm." He
spoke on the assumption that after we had given up
our arms the rest of the nations would continue to
arm—if not with their own money, then with the
millions wrung from the completely disarmed German
nation. Whilst opposing the propaganda of the S.P.D.
and Centre in favour of signing the Treaty, he
prophesied that the Ruhr would be occupied, whatever we signed.

1921

This year was marked by the foundation of the first
local groups of Rosenheim and Landshut. Hitler
organized the first body of men to protect the
Party, and began his fight against the Separatist
movement in Bavaria. Our leader also addressed
a meeting of over five thousand in the Circus in
Munich.

He declared at his meetings that fulfilment of the
Treaty would not help, as the S.D.P., Centre, and
Volkspartei asserted, to build up German prosperity
in peace and quiet, but that the result of this foolish
policy was bound to be inflation on a large scale,
involving immense injury to German industry.
Hitler's assertion that the Black-Red Government
was planning to denationalize the State Railways was
declared to be a "bare-faced lie." An attempt at a

revolt within the Party was defeated. Hitler drafted the new Constitution of the Party, which gave him dictatorial powers.

Social Democracy, which could not continue to ignore the name of Hitler, now attempted to get rid of its bugbear by methods of terrorism. There were sanguinary collisions at the meetings, in which our leader's iron nerves maintained the upper hand. An invincible bodyguard was formed, which thenceforward was known as the "Storm Detachment."

1922

While the conquest of Munich was proceeding, the movement was beginning to spread through the rest of Bavaria. Hitler rejected all overtures, by way of compromise, to join up with other Parties. He gradually destroyed all similar "nationalist" Party formations, and made the National Socialist movement supreme over them.

In October 1922 Hitler marched at the head of eight hundred men to Coburg, and within forty-eight hours had utterly crushed the Red Terror in that city.

Adolf Hitler then declared publicly that we were rushing headlong in the direction of inflation, which he had foreseen as the result of the policy of the Black-Red coalition. He became known as the most dangerous and best hated enemy of the system. Social Democracy and the Centre Party ceased to defend themselves by argument, and adopted a policy of defamation.

1923

In January 1923 the first great Party Conference was held, and the first banners of the Party were consecrated. The Storm Detachment was formally incorporated.

The Party propaganda was exhaustively studied and improved, and the permanent principles of the organization were settled and established. Adherents gathered round Hitler in large numbers, the majority of whom are today his steadfast partners in the struggle. The attacks upon him were meanwhile pursued with increasing determination; he found himself in prison for the first time, on the charge of disturbing the meetings of his adversaries; and he was repeatedly fined. Nevertheless, he never for one moment ceased fighting against the system.

During the summer of 1923 Adolf Hitler proceeded to break down the Red Terror in the majority of the Bavarian cities—Ratisbon, Hof, Bayreuth, Nuremberg, Furth, Ingolstadt, Wirzburg, Schweinfurt—often at the cost of street fighting and bloodshed, in which he defeated the Social-Democratic and Communist terrorists.

His struggle against the incompetent Government of the Reich was accompanied by bitter accusations. He prophesied the ill-success of the Government's feeble resistance in the matter of the Ruhr, and constantly attacked the stupid policy of submitting to the French dictate, and the policy of fulfilment. He never failed to point to the necessity of an understanding with England and Italy.

In November 1923 Adolf Hitler made his attempt to overthrow the system. The rising failed, and Hitler was arrested.

1924

The great Trial took place in Munich, 1924. Though found guilty on the facts, our leader achieved an overwhelming moral justification. Hitler's defence influenced the Court to such an extent, and his assumption of sole and exclusive responsibility was so convincing, that the speech of the counsel for the prosecution was actually a remarkable testimony to his honourable motives. The judge, however, condemned him to a period of detention.

The National Socialist Party suffered by the loss of its leader. Its adversaries were convinced that the movement was shattered, and plucked up courage to sign the infamous Dawes Pact, thus deliberately starting the system of plundering Germany which was brought to a head in the Young Plan. The objective of the enslavement of Germany was apparently achieved. What a triumph for the Social Democrats and the Centre!

In vain Hitler tried, through his associates, who were at liberty, to put up a fight against the Dawes Pact. In vain he made them declare in public that the Centre Party, the S.D.P., and the Volkspartei, in declaring that the foreign loans under the Plan would increase national prosperity, that unemployment would cease, that wages would be raised and taxes reduced, and that agriculture would be saved, were merely deceiving the nation. In vain he made them point out that the Dawes Pact was bound to increase poverty, since the interest on the loans would cripple industry, while the loans themselves merely served the purpose of fulfilling the financial obligations under the Plan; bankruptcy and unemployment would increase, wages would sink, prices and taxation would rise still further, and the farmers would be faced with utter ruin, and be forced to part with all they possessed.

On December 20th Hitler quitted the fortress in which he had been detained.

1925

On February 27, 1925, Adolf Hitler's call for the re-birth of the Party was published, and he made his first speech after his confinement before an audience of four thousand persons.

The National Socialist movement had been broken up after the events of November 9th, and all its property and its funds had been confiscated; so that Adolf Hitler now started with nothing in hand to rebuild the Party from its foundations. *Vorwärts* and *Germania*, in Berlin, ridiculed his efforts, and mocked at the "fool whom imprisonment had made mad." Nevertheless, the reconstruction of the Party proceeded with great rapidity under Hitler's leadership. The old leaders gathered faithfully round him once more. Hitler stimulated the Party Press into fresh activity.

By December 1925 the Party numbered 27,000 members.

The Centre and the Social Democrats, in their alarm, decreed that the leader should not speak in public for two years.

1926

June of this year saw the first Conference of the Party since Hitler's imprisonment.

The bourgeois world was still convinced that the policy of fulfilment would save Germany, and that the Dawes Pact would revive industry. The Marxists were convinced that their domination was unshakable.

President von Hindenburg separated himself from his supporters and marched off with the Centre and the S.D.P.

The Party carried on the struggle; by the end of the year it numbered 49,000 members.

1927

The order forbidding Hitler to speak in public was withdrawn, since it was found impossible to enforce it. He addressed numbers of mass meetings. Each month saw the Party more and more firmly consolidated.

Developments on all sides proved more and more convincingly that Hitler had been right. The Dawes Pact was unmasked, and the consequences were terrific. The Social Democrats and the Centre Party attempted to save what could be saved by means of lies and abuse.

In August Hitler summoned a Party Conference at Nuremberg, which proved a great success. By the end of the year the Party numbered 72,000 members.

1928

Adolf Hitler led his Party in an intensified assault on the existing system. National Socialism was now the inexorable enemy of the destroyers of Germany within and without. Hitler directed his attack especially against the senseless manner in which the farmers and the middle classes were being ruined. He prophesied the catastrophe which would fall upon the home markets. He declared, at hundreds of meetings, again and again, that the policy of fulfilment was lunacy, and that its consequences would mean death and ruin to German industry. The Social Democrats and Centre mocked and jeered in their attempt to revenge themselves. Their lies and abuse were directed at Hitler personally.

By the end of the year twelve members of the Party sat in the Reichstag, and its strength had increased to 108,000.

1929

Adolf Hitler continued to fight the existing system with unflagging energy. The Press of the Party was perfected, the Storm Detachment increased, the S.S. formations strengthened, and the propaganda intensified. The doctrines of National Socialism began to penetrate deeply into the national consciousness.

On August 4th the second Party Conference was held at Nuremberg. Hitler attacked the Black-Red system with ever increasing energy, and stood forth without a rival, as the most powerful of the nation's leaders against all that was meant by "Democracy." All attempts to oust him from the leadership of the Party were crushed.

By the end of the year the Party numbered 179,000 members.

1930

The struggle against the Young Plan was in full swing. Hindenburg defended it with energy, asserting that by it Germany would be saved, that German industry would revive, that unemployment would be stemmed, that the farmers would breathe again, and that it would be possible to lighten taxation.

Adolf Hitler described such views as unreal and disastrous; he prophesied the very contrary. His Party proceeded to enlighten the nation, amidst severe conflicts. Its opponents replied with a torrent of lies.

The elections to the Reichstag took place on September 14, 1930. The Party polled $6\frac{1}{2}$ million votes, and 107 members were elected. Its internal organization was stronger than ever. A few minor attempts at revolt, promoted from outside, were promptly crushed by Hitler, and those who would not submit unconditionally were expelled.

The Centre Party, which had now delivered itself into the hands of the S.P.D. for good or ill, began to incite the Church against Hitler. Bishops and priests, belonging to the Centre Party, started a fanatical attack upon the National Socialist movement, excommunicated its adherents, and even refused them Christian burial. Hitler held unshakably to his conviction that the Centre spelt ruin for Germany, and continued his fight against it with even greater determination than before. He sternly rejected any attempt to extort from him some modification of his opinions.

By the end of the year the Party numbered 389,000 members.

1931

The fight against the Young Plan continued. The consequences foreseen by Hitler became a reality.

The Government began to administrate by means of emergency measures, thinking thus to save industry. Sharp disputes followed, in which Adolf Hitler once more pointed out the fatal consequences of that policy. In a few months—a few weeks even—he was proved to be right.

Meanwhile numbers of National Socialist newspapers had sprung up, and the central publishing office of the Party had gradually grown to be a vast enterprise. The Party organization had become highly efficient, and the Storm Detachment had reached a high stage of development.

Our opponents, wallowing in lies, were allowing orders for goods to be placed in France.

By the end of the year 1931 the membership of the Hitler Party attained to 806,000, a month later to 862,000, and again a month later to 920,000. On the day of the Election there were something like 1,000,000 members, and untold millions of supporters at the polls.

The man who was once a poor worker, and later a soldier at the front, had thus in barely thirteen years built up the greatest political organization which Germany has ever seen. The only resources which his opponents can employ against this man are lies and defamation. And he has always won so far, in spite of all the lies, and this time he has come near to being elected President of the Reich.

1933

It is beyond question that Adolf Hitler is the ablest politician who has ever occupied the Federal Chancellery. During the whole of the struggle of the National Socialist Party Adolf Hitler has proved that in national and foreign policy he has an eye for facts. His conduct and his speech are those of a man who is sure of his aim. Thanks to the overwhelming support given to him by the elections of March 5th and November 12th, the Reichskanzler Adolf Hitler was able so to integrate and unite the political parties and provinces of Germany that she will now be able to solve her internal difficulties and once more secure full equality in the family of nations.

Since Adolf Hitler's accession to power he has displayed such outstanding ability as politician and leader that he is destined to become Germany's greatest reformer in social, economic and political reconstruction.

The German people have absolute faith in Adolf Hitler, and are convinced that as through Hitler the National Socialist Movement, in fourteen years of heroic and spiritual struggle, gradually conquered all true-hearted Germans, so the National Socialist Germany, through Hitler, will win the confidence, esteem and appreciation of other nations.

I

OFFICIAL PARTY MANIFESTO

ON THE POSITION OF THE N.S.D.A.P. WITH REGARD TO
THE FARMING POPULATION AND AGRICULTURE

MUNICH, MARCH 6, 1930

1. IMPORTANCE OF THE FARMING CLASS AND OF AGRICULTURE TO THE GERMAN PEOPLE

The German nation obtains a considerable portion of its food by the importation of foreign foodstuffs. Before the World War we were able to pay for these imports with our industrial exports, our trade, and our deposits of capital abroad. The outcome of the war put an end to this possibility.

Today we are paying for our imported food mostly with the help of foreign loans, which drive the German nation deeper and deeper into debt-slavery to the international financiers who provide credits. If things go on as they are the German people will become more and more impoverished. The financiers, by cutting off their credits, and therefore the imports of foodstuffs—that is, by hanging the bread-bin out of reach—can, above all, compel the German proletarians to work in their service for starvation wages, or to allow themselves to be shipped as wage-slaves to foreign colonies.

The only possibility of escaping from this thraldom

lies in the ability of Germany to produce essential foodstuffs at home. *The increased production of German agriculture is therefore a question of life and death for the German nation.*

Moreover, a rural population, economically sound, with abundant purchasing power, is essential to our industry, which will in future have to look for more and more openings in the home market.

We not only recognize the predominant importance of the working classes for our nation, but we also see in the rural population, as the principal bearers of the nation's inheritance of health, the source of the nation's youth, and the backbone of its defensive forces.

The maintenance of an efficient agricultural class, increasing in numbers as the general population increases, is a cornerstone of the National Socialist policy, since this is directed towards the welfare of all our people in the generations to come.

2. NEGLECT OF THE FARMING CLASS AND OF AGRICULTURE IN THE PRESENT GERMAN STATE

By disregard of the biological and economic importance of the farming population, and by opposition to the vitally necessary demand for increased agricultural production, the maintenance of an economically sound farming population in the German State is today seriously threatened.

The considerable increase in agricultural production which is in itself quite possible is being hindered by the fact that owing to their increasing indebtedness the farmers are unable to acquire the necessary stock, and because the stimulus to increased production is lacking, since farming no longer pays.

The reasons why farming is no longer profitable are to be sought:

1. In the existing *fiscal policy*, which lays excessive burdens on agriculture. This is due to Party considerations, and because the Jewish world money-market—which actually controls parliamentary democracy in Germany—wishes to destroy German agriculture, since this would place the German nation, and especially the working class, completely at its mercy;

2. In the competition of foreign agriculture, which enjoys more favourable conditions, and is insufficiently checked by the fiscal policy, which is hostile to German agriculture;

3. In the extravagant profits of wholesale trade, which thrusts itself in between the producer and consumer of agricultural produce, and of which the greater part is today in the hands of the Jews;

4. In the oppressive rates which the farmer has to pay for electric power and artificial manures to concerns mainly run by Jews.

The high taxation cannot be met out of the poor returns for labour on the land. The farmer is forced to run into debt and to pay usurious interest for loans. He sinks deeper and deeper under this tyranny, and in the end forfeits house and farm to the money-lender, who is usually a Jew.

The German farming population is being expropriated.

3. IN THE REICH OF THE FUTURE FOR WHICH WE ARE
   WORKING THE RIGHTS OF THE GERMAN SOIL WILL
   BE RESPECTED AND THERE WILL BE A GERMAN
   AGRICULTURAL POLICY

There can be no hope of any sweeping improvement
in the desperate position of the rural population, or
of a revival of agriculture, as long as the German
Government is in fact controlled by the international
money-magnates, with the help of the parliamentary-
democratic system of government, since they wish
to destroy the national strength of Germany.

In the new and very different German State to which
we aspire the farming population and agriculture will
receive the consideration due to their importance as
the main support of a truly national German State.

From this emerge the following requirements:

1. The soil of Germany, acquired and defended by
the German people, serves the German nation as a
home and as a means of livelihood. It must be administered in this sense by the individual owner of the soil.

2. Only members of the German nation may possess
land.

3. Land legally acquired by them shall be regarded
as inheritable property. To the right to hold property,
however, is attached the obligation to use it in the
national interest. Special courts shall be appointed
to supervise this obligation; these shall consist of
representatives from all departments of the land-
holding class, and one representative of the State.

4. German soil may not become an object of financial speculation (cf. Point 17, p. 41), nor may it provide an unearned income for its owner. It may be acquired only by him who is prepared to cultivate it himself. Therefore the State has a right of pre-emption on every sale of land.

It is forbidden to pledge land to private lenders. The necessary loans for cultivation will be granted to farmers for cultivation either by associations recognized by the State, or by the State itself.

5. Dues will be paid to the State for the use of land according to the extent and quality of the property. By this tax on the produce of the soil any further taxation of agricultural land or agriculture will be obviated.

6. No hard and fast rule can be laid down as to the size of agricultural holdings. From the point of view of our population policy large numbers of prosperous small- and middle-sized farms are all-important. Farming on a large scale, however, has its special and *necessary* part to play, and if it preserves a sound relation towards the smaller farms it is justifiable.

7. The inheritance of landed property will be so regulated by a law of inheritance as to prevent sub-division of property and the accumulation of debt upon it.

8. The State has the right to confiscate, on payment of adequate indemnity:

(*a*) Land which is not in the possession of German nationals;

(*b*) Land which—according to the judgment of the competent land court—is no longer serving

C

towards the maintenance of the people, owing to bad and irresponsible exploitation;

(c) Parts of large estates not exploited by the owner himself, for the purpose of settling a free peasantry;

(d) Land required for special State purposes in the interests of the community as a whole (e.g. for communications and national defence).

Land acquired illegally (according to German law) may be confiscated without compensation.

9. It is the duty of the State to settle such land as becomes available, on methodical lines, in accordance with a general population policy.

The land shall be allotted to settlers as a hereditary possession under conditions which shall make a livelihood possible.

Settlers shall be selected by examination as to their civic and professional suitability. Special favour shall be shown to sons of farmers who have not the right to inherit (see § 7).

The colonization of the Eastern frontiers is of predominant importance. In this case the mere establishment of farms will not be sufficient, but it will be necessary to develop country towns in connection with the new branch of industry. This is the only way to provide marketing possibilities which will make the smaller farms a paying proposition.

It will be the duty of Germany's foreign policy to provide large spaces for the nourishment and settlement of the growing population of Germany.

4. THE FARMING CLASS MUST BE UPLIFTED ECONO-MICALLY AND EDUCATIONALLY

It is the duty of the State to promote the economic and cultural uplifting of the farming population, conformably with its importance to the nation as a whole, and thereby to remove one of the chief causes of the flight from the land.

1. The present poverty of the land population must be at once relieved by remissions of taxation and other special measures. Further indebtedness must be checked by statutory reduction of the rate of interest on loans to that of the pre-war period, and by summary action against extortionate creditors.

2. It must be the State's agricultural policy to see to it that farming be made to pay once more.

German agriculture must be protected by tariffs, State regulation of imports, and a scheme of national training.

The fixing of prices for agricultural produce must be withdrawn from the influence of Stock Exchange speculation, and a stop must be put to the exploitation of the agricultural interest by the large middlemen, the transfer of whose business to agricultural co-operative associations must be encouraged by the State.

It shall be the task of such professional organizations to reduce the running expenses of farmers and increase production. (Provision of implements, manures, seed and breeding stock, on favourable conditions, improvements, war against vermin, free advice, chemical research, etc.) The State shall provide generous assistance to the professional organizations in carrying out their task. In particular the State must insist on a considerable reduction in the cost to farmers of artificial manures and electric power.

3. It will also be the duty of the professional organizations to establish the class of farm labourers as members of the farming community by contracts which are socially just. Supervision and arbitration in these matters will be the function of the State.

It must be made possible for good labourers to rise to the status of farm-owners.

The necessary improvements in living conditions and wages of farm labourers will ensue as soon as the general farming situation improves. When these conditions take a turn for the better it will be no longer necessary to employ foreign labour on the land, and this custom will in future be forbidden.

4. The National importance of the farming class requires that the State shall promote technical education in agriculture. (Homes for children of farmers, agricultural high-schools, with very favourable terms for talented boys without means.)

5. PROFESSIONAL AGRICULTURAL ORGANIZATIONS CANNOT PROVIDE ALL THE ASSISTANCE REQUIRED BY THE FARMING CLASS. ONLY THE POLITICAL LIBERATION MOVEMENT OF THE N.S.D.A.P. CAN DO THIS

The rural population are poor because the whole German nation is poor. It is an error to imagine that one single class of workers can escape sharing the fortunes of the German community as a whole—and a crime to incite jealousy between the rural population and the cities, as these are bound together for good or ill.

Economic assistance under the present political system cannot produce any sweeping improvement, for the poverty of the German people is rooted in its political enslavement, from which only political means can liberate it. The old political Parties, which were, and are, responsible for the national enslavement, cannot be our leaders on the road to freedom.

There are important economic tasks awaiting professional organizations in our future State; even now they can do much preparatory work in that direction; but they are not adapted to the political struggle of liberation which is to lay the foundation of a new economic order; since that battle will have to be fought not from the point of view of a single profession, but from that of the whole nation.

The battle for freedom against our oppressors and their taskmasters can be fought successfully only by a political movement of liberation, comprising the German-conscious of all ranks and classes, and fully acknowledging the importance of the rural population and agriculture for the nation as a whole.

This political liberation movement of the German people is the N.S.D.A.P.

(*Signed*) ADOLF HITLER.

II

THE 25 POINTS

The National Socialist German Workers' Party—
registered as the "National-Socialist German Workers'
Union"—at a great mass meeting on February 25,
1920, in the Hofbrauähus-Festsaal in Munich,
announced its Programme to the world.

In Section 2 of the Constitution of our Party this
Programme is declared to be unalterable. It is as
follows:

THE PROGRAMME

The Programme of the German Workers' Party is
limited as to period. The leaders have no intention,
once the aims announced in it have been achieved, of
setting up fresh ones, in order to ensure the continued
existence of the Party by the artificially increased
discontent of the masses.

1. We demand the union of all Germans, on the
basis of the right of the self-determination of peoples,
to form a Great Germany.

2. We demand equality of rights for the German
People in its dealings with other nations, and abolition
of the Peace Treaties of Versailles and St. Germain.

3. We demand land and territory (colonies) for the
nourishment of our people and for settling our surplus
population.

4. None but members of the nation may be citizens of the State. None but those of German blood, whatever their creed, may be members of the nation. No Jew, therefore, may be a member of the nation.

5. Anyone who is not a citizen of the State may live in Germany only as a guest and must be regarded as being subject to the Alien laws.

6. The right of voting on the leadership and legislation is to be enjoyed by the citizens of the State alone. We demand therefore that all official appointments, of whatever kind, whether in the Reich, the provinces, or the small communities, shall be granted to citizens of the State alone.

We oppose the corrupt Parliamentary custom of the State of filling posts merely with a view to Party considerations, and without reference to character or capacity.

7. We demand that the State shall make it its first duty to promote the industry and livelihood of the citizens of the State. If it is not possible to nourish the entire population of the State, foreign nationals (non-citizens of the State) must be excluded from the Reich.

8. All further non-German immigration must be prevented. We demand that all non-Germans who entered Germany subsequently to August 2, 1914, shall be required forthwith to depart from the Reich.

9. All citizens of the State shall possess equal rights and duties.

10. It must be the first duty of every citizen of the

State to perform mental or physical work. The activities of the individual must not clash with the interests of the whole, but must proceed within the framework of the community and must be for the general good.

We demand therefore:

11. Abolition of incomes unearned by work.

ABOLITION OF THE THRALDOM OF INTEREST

12. In view of the enormous sacrifice of life and property demanded of a nation by every war, personal enrichment through war must be regarded as a crime against the nation. We demand therefore the ruthless confiscation of all war profits.

13. We demand the nationalization of all businesses which have (hitherto) been amalgamated (into Trusts).

14. We demand that there shall be profit-sharing in the great industries.

15. We demand a generous development of provision for old age.

16. We demand the creation and maintenance of a healthy middle class, immediate communalization of wholesale warehouses, and their lease at a low rate to small traders, and that the most careful consideration shall be shown to all small purveyors to the State, the provinces, or smaller communities.

17. We demand a land-reform suitable to our national requirements, the passing of a law for the confiscation without compensation of land for communal purposes,

the abolition of interest on mortgages, and prohibition of all speculation in land.[1]

18. We demand ruthless war upon all those whose activities are injurious to the common interest. Common criminals against the nation, usurers, profiteers, etc., must be punished with death, whatever their creed or race.

19. We demand that the Roman Law, which serves the materialistic world order, shall be replaced by a German common law.

20. With the aim of opening to every capable and industrious German the possibility of higher education and consequent advancement to leading positions the State must consider a thorough re-construction of our national system of education. The curriculum of all educational establishments must be brought into line with the requirements of practical life. Directly

---

[1] On April 13, 1928, Adolf Hitler made the following declaration:

"It is necessary to reply to the false interpretation on the part of our opponents of Point 17 of the Programme of the N.S.D.A.P.

"Since the N.S.D.A.P. admits the principle of private property, it is obvious that the expression 'confiscation without compensation' refers merely to the creation of possible legal means of confiscating, when necessary, land illegally acquired, or not administered in accordance with the national welfare. It is therefore directed in the first instance against the Jewish companies which speculate in land.

"(*Signed*) ADOLF HITLER.

"MUNICH, *April* 13, 1928."

the mind begins to develop the schools must aim at teaching the pupil to understand the idea of the State (State sociology). We demand the education of specially gifted children of poor parents, whatever their class or occupation, at the expense of the State.

21. The State must apply itself to raising the standard of health in the nation by protecting mothers and infants, prohibiting child labour, and increasing bodily efficiency by legally obligatory gymnastics and sports, and by extensive support of clubs engaged in the physical training of the young.

22. We demand the abolition of mercenary troops and the formation of a national army.

23. We demand legal warfare against conscious political lies and their dissemination in the Press. In order to facilitate the creation of a German national Press we demand:

(a) That all editors of and contributors to newspapers employing the German language must be members of the nation;

(b) That special permission from the State shall be necessary before non-German newspapers may appear. These need not necessarily be printed in the German language;

(c) That non-Germans shall be prohibited by law from participating financially in or influencing German newspapers, and that the penalty for contravention of the law shall be suppression of any such newspaper, and immediate deportation of the non-German involved.

It must be forbidden to publish newspapers which do not conduce to the national welfare. We demand the legal prosecution of all tendencies in art and literature of a kind likely to disintegrate our life as a nation, and the suppression of institutions which militate against the above-mentioned requirements.

24. We demand liberty for all religious denominations in the State, so far as they are not a danger to it and do not militate against the morality and moral sense of the German race.

The Party, as such, stands for positive Christianity, but does not bind itself in the matter of creed to any particular confession. It combats the Jewish-materialist spirit *within* and *without* us, and is convinced that our nation can achieve permanent health from within only on the principle:

THE COMMON INTEREST BEFORE SELF-INTEREST

25. That all the foregoing requirements may be realized we demand the creation of a strong central power of the Reich. Unconditional authority of the politically central Parliament over the entire Reich and its organization in general.

The formation of Diets and vocational Chambers for the purpose of executing the general laws promulgated by the Reich in the various States of the Confederation.

The leaders of the Party swear to proceed regardless of consequences—if necessary at the sacrifice of their lives—towards the fulfilment of the foregoing Points.

MUNICH, *February* 24, 1920.

After full discussion at the General Meeting of members on May 22, 1920, it was resolved that "This Programme is unalterable." This does not imply that every word must stand unchanged, nor that any efforts to extend or develop the Programme are to be prohibited, but it does imply that the principles and basic ideas contained in it are not to be tampered with.

There can be no twisting and turning for reasons of expediency, no secret meddling with the most important—and for the present order of politics, society, and economics, most unwelcome—points in the Programme; no deviation from its original sense.

Adolf Hitler has emphasized the two cornerstones of the programme by printing them in heavy type:

The Common Interest before Self-Interest —that is the Spirit of the Programme.

Abolition of the Thraldom of Interest— that is the Kernel of National Socialism.

The achievement of these two points means the victory of the approaching universalist order of society of the "true State" over the present disintegration of State, nation, and economy under the corrupting influence of the individualist theory of society now obtaining. The sham State of today, oppressing the working classes and protecting the pirated gains of bankers and Stock Exchange speculators, is the arena for the most reckless private enrichment and the lowest political profiteering; it gives no thought to its people, and provides no high moral bond of union.

The power of money, most brutal of all powers, holds absolute sway, and exercises a corrupting and destroying influence on State, nation, society, morals, drama, and literature, and on all moral imponderables.

There must of course be no wavering, no drawing back in this battle of giants; it is either victory or extinction.

A slightly different conception of precisely the same fundamental ideas, such as I have given in my book, *Der deutsche Staat auf nationaler und sozialer Grundlage* (F. Eher Nachf.,) is not an alteration, but merely a particular arrangement and summation of various related points in accordance with the various political, economic, financial, and cultural spheres of life.

If this conception of mine (see p. 22) could be regarded as differing from or opposed to the 25 Points, Hitler would never have described my book in his brief, concise preface as "the catechism of our movement." Anyone is free to choose either of these conceptions, according to his taste, but if he compares them he will not find them mutually contradictory.

In order to insure for the future absolute agreement in our demands as expressed in our Programme, and to guard the movement against the shocks likely to injure any movement—the "suggestions for improvement" offered by qualified and unqualified critics, grumblers, and know-alls—Adolf Hitler, at a conference of all district organizers held at Bamberg on February 14, 1923, formally appointed Gottfried Feder to be the final judge of all questions connected with the Programme.

III

THE BASIC IDEAS

It cannot be the task of this pamphlet to deal exhaustively with the sociological and philosophical, the spiritual and structural bases of the National Socialist concept of the State. This will be the special task of a later volume of this series; but in these pages our intention is merely to expound, as simply and directly as possible, the essential and basic ideas underlying this concept.

Nor can we here attempt to describe the various other political tendencies, nor those who represent them in the different parties and associations—this too will be the task of a special volume—but shall merely make a preliminary statement of the essential points of our demands.

The world arose from chaos, order from disorder, organic life from the raving vortex.

Today chaos is rampant in the world—confusion, conflict, hatred, oppression, robbery, cruelty, self-seeking. Brother is estranged from brother. Members of the same nation attack one another, and club a man to death simply because he wears a Swastika. They all suffer under the same burdens, the same privations; yet who during these last months has ever heard of Marxist workers attacking and beating their employers to death, or their Party leaders, or even one of the Bank and Stock Exchange blood-suckers, or a wholesale profiteer? The victims of chaos are the simple, honest workers. Men's minds are confused; the Marxists are flocking round the greatest exploiters of their own class, while they turn savagely against those who stand ready to rescue it.

The Nationalists, the members of the Fatherland Party, and of the Right, are aiming at entering the Government, or are co-operating in it with those who deny and destroy their ideal of the State, losing thereby both honour and character. The defence associations are striving to penetrate "into the State"—the State of Severing and Grzesinsky—believing that they can govern the country in association with pacifists, internationalists, and Jews.

Men's minds are confused! The so-called *Rechtskreise* fail to see that there can never be friendship and co-operation between eagles and snakes, wolves and lambs, mankind and the cholera bacillus. With all their might, with their "will to form," they are supporting "order" grown disorder, political chaos, political effeteness. But they opposed the National Socialists, those "fanatics," repudiated, as alleged "realistic politicians," the saviours of their country from political chaos, hating them, although feeling themselves akin to them—filled with crazy anxiety lest the National Socialists should deprive them of some of their former posts or privileges—forgetting that they had lost everything through the very people from whom they now demand a share in the political loaves and fishes of the State!

The industrialists, great or small, have but one end in view—profits: only one desire—credits: only one protest—against taxation; they fear and respect only one thing—the banks; they have only a supercilious shrug of the shoulders for the National Socialist demand for the abolition of the thraldom of interest.

Their one desire is to "make debts." The vast tribute extracted from loans by the banks, without trouble or labour, they regard as perfectly in order. They found their own "Parties of Economy," and vote for the Dawes Laws, which are the main cause of the heavy taxation.

They hurl themselves into the depths of interest-slavery, complain of the taxes and rates of interest, and swoon with respect before every banker or Stock Exchange pirate. Men's minds are confused. The whole economy of the country is degraded, depersonalized, transformed into joint-stock companies. The producers have surrendered to high finance, their greatest enemy. The employers in factories and offices, deeply in debt, have to be content with the barest pittance, for all the profits of labour go into the pockets of the impersonal money power in the form of interest and dividends.

The people who have taken control of the national economy are totally unable to stem the chaos. Crushed from above by taxation and interest, menaced from below by the subterranean grumblings of the workers, they have blindly and crazily flung themselves into the arms of capitalistic finance and its "State," and are tolerated by the exploiters and profiteers of the existing chaos merely as the slave-drivers set over the labouring masses. Their fury is directed not against the butchers of German economy, not against the lunacy of Marxism, but against the wearers of the Hooked Cross. They forget that we and we alone saw the tragedy of German economics approaching, foretold it, and showed how, if taken in time, Germany by her own strength could recover her equilibrium.

Associations, representatives of interests, unions of professional men, officials, clerks, societies of small investors or Reichsbank creditors, defence associations, Front Fighters' associations, farmers' unions, landowners' unions, trade unions, brotherhoods, clubs, or whatever such curious organizations may call themselves—reasonable enough in their basic ideas, but hopeless in the present chaos of public life—are seeking to evoke order. In vain, for they are not in touch with the nation as a great social whole. All are intent merely on snatching small advantages for their own caste, their own class; barren of any political or economic principle, they apply to each political Party in turn. They bow to the existing system, and kow-tow to the so-called supreme authority.

They cost the German nation untold sums in payments to numberless organizers, syndics, directors, and wire-pullers, but none of them do any good. Inflation —a criminal revolutionary measure—robs all classes of their savings—thrifty investors, trade unions, and

D

artisans. A fiscal law, concocted in a Government office, destroys the hopes based on years of work. An advantage gained by the one side after numberless meetings, discussions, and deputations to the Government, is usually annulled by a rise in the cost of living, a rise or a fall of prices.

Chaos and lunacy! Men's minds are confused. How can a farmer live when he is flayed and pestered? How can the worker buy with prices raised by the middleman? What use is it at last to raise the pay of officials and employees when the index of the cost of living continues to rise ever higher? They look in their credulity for help from the State, the State which has impoverished and repressed the people, which is not the "Father of the Nation," but the tyrant and tax-collector of the money despotism.

So they turn once again to the old Parties; they say they don't care for politics, and belong to no Party, and at the same time they let the wretched Party squabbles go on as before.

We see the same frightful picture of chaos in all the other manifestations of public life, whether in art, literature, the theatre, the cinema, the radio, the church, the schools; everywhere is the "ferment of decomposition," the great wrecker and destroyer, the Jew and the Freemason, filling the most important posts, or working invisibly behind the scenes, pulling the strings of his puppets, who dance on the public stage as a Stresemann or a Scheidemann, or openly, as Jakob Goldschmidt, Warburg, Wassermann, Levy, etc., bleed and exploit the German people through the Press and the scourge of interest.

The great task which National Socialism has set before it is a determination to restore form, to dispel the chaos, to set the disjointed world in order again, and to act as the guardian—in the highest Platonic sense—of that order.

It should be stated here that we regard as "Order" neither the apparent external order of a policed State, nor the robbery of finance hallowed by custom and permitted by law, nor the agreements of syndicates, trusts, and other organized measures of national betrayal, however well they "function." Even a band of robbers has "order," and prisons have their "regulations." But in the nation, taken as an organic whole, almost every aspect of our public life shows misery, bondage, suppression, and insincerity, and presents a chaotic picture of the struggle of all against all.

We see Government *versus* people, Party *versus* Party, at the same time concluding the most strange and impossible alliances; employer *versus* employee, merchant *versus* producer and consumer, landlord *versus* tenant, labourer *versus* farmer, officials *versus* the public, worker *versus* "bourgeoisie," Church *versus* State, each blindly hitting out at his particular adversary, and thinking only of his own selfish interests, his advancement, and his money-bags. No one reflects that the other man has a right to live, or that the pursuit of his own selfish ends means that someone else has to pay. No one thinks of his neighbour's welfare, or of his higher duties to the community. A breathless chase after personal gain. Elbow your neighbour to get on, trample on his body if you will get anything by it—who cares? That is the spirit of modern business.

So the many shriek and bellow and run hither and thither; so the stronger pulls and pushes the weaker, kicks him, and strikes him to the ground; so the base man serves the worthy, the brutal man the noble; the lust of enjoyment destroys morality, violence triumphs over right, Party interests over the general welfare. Rascality, speculation, and fraud triumph over honest work.

So terrible a battle of all the baser instincts was never yet known. One is involuntarily tempted to recall the old prophecy of the Twilight of the Gods: "then right and seemly conduct perish; the time of the wolf and the axe sets in; the sea rages, fire falls from heaven, and gods and men pass away."

Let us not deceive ourselves. We are in the midst of a great world change, and it is natural that the simple soul, the poor bewildered spirit, sees no way out of the chaos, and seeks relief in suicide, or thinks the world is coming to an end, joins in the race after the golden calf, and rushes blindly into the crazy vortex. "Enjoy while you can—after us the deluge."

So terrible a blow to the morale of a nation is possible and explicable only when the whole intellectual foundation of society is false or tottering—and in fact we see that Marxists, Capitalists, and the leaders of our public life all worship the same god—*Individualism. Personal interest is the sole incentive*—the advantage of one's own narrow class the sole aim in life.

Here again I must refer to a further contribution to this series, devoted to a careful sociological study of the structure of society.

Here I shall attempt only in passing to give a comparative picture of the fundamental difference between the organic structure—or the lack of it—in the present State and the political economy of today, and the essence of a National Socialist State. The current doctrine is: Society is the sum of individuals—the State at its best a convenient aggregation of individuals or associations.

We may compare this doctrine of the construction of society to a *heap of stones*. The only real thing about it is the individual pieces of stone. Its shape is a matter of chance; whether a stone is on top or underneath is indifferent. The result is neither more nor less than a heap of stones.

By the same simile, the State which answers to our National Socialist doctrine of society and philosophy of the State is the house. Speaking mechanically, the house also consists of so many individual items— bricks, sand, cement, joists, windows, doors, floors, etc. But anyone can see that a house, a room, is a higher entity, something new and peculiar and complete in itself, something more than a mere sum total of bricks heaped together. Anyone can understand that a house does not come into being by piling a number of single parts in a heap, but only by assembling these parts according to a deliberate plan. Then only do we obtain something new, something greater, the spiritual super-structure, so to speak.

Thus it is with the nation. Not until chaos has been reduced to deliberate and organic order, not until chaos gives place to definite and planned form, not until the individual components begin to live a real and purposeful life, can *the true State* appear. Othmar Spann, formerly Rector of Vienna University, has admirably expounded in his book, *Der wahre Staat*, and in his *Gesellschaftslehre*, the sociological bases of the modern individualistic State as opposed to the high ideal of universal order in a State founded on scientific principles.

We National Socialists have coined the simple phrase, which all can understand:

The Common Interest before Self-Interest

Only in the service of the whole community, only as a useful and active member within the framework of the national community, does the individual awake to the higher life; only so does everyone—each in his own place—become truly of one substance with the higher totality of his nation; only when *thus* understood does the real Socialism —the *sense of community* —take on true life. Only under the governance of this basic idea will the individual enjoy a sense of security, and realize that only under this controlling idea can a manifold and organic national economy emerge from the robber-economy of the present day, for the benefit of the whole community—and therefore for the benefit of every individual.

Today the individual is a helpless victim of the forces fighting for the mastery; his associations are powerless to help him. It is not clearly realized who is the real enemy—the idle profiteer and exploiter.

In spite of the Marxist outcry against capitalism, the pious pronouncements of the Centre, and the complaints of the business world of the burden of taxation and interest, no one realizes who is the world-enemy—the capitalistic finance which over-shadows the world, and its representative, the Jew.

All classes of the people have felt the scourge of interest; the tax-collector bears heavily on every section of the population—but who dares oppose the supreme power of Bank and Stock Exchange? Capital proclaims its character by growing, contrary to all experience elsewhere on earth, without pains or labour, by means of interest and dividends, waxing greater and more powerful each minute. The devilish principle of falsehood has triumphed over the ordered principle of creative labour.

ABOLISH THE THRALDOM OF INTEREST IS OUR WAR-CRY

I know that this demand, which underlies every other, is not properly understood in its vast significance, even in our own ranks. We see, for example, that very few of our speakers dare to attack this basic question, though most of them feel how important it is; for one of our Party slogans is "War upon the Stock Exchanges and capital loans!" But what the "thraldom of interest" really is, how in practice it weighs upon the life of the nation and the individual, by what technical methods "finance" has enslaved the population, what the right and practical methods are which must be adopted to break it, and what the results of breaking it would be for the whole population—to very few is this so clear that they can explain it in their own words.

In his fundamental work, *Mein Kampf* (vol. i, pp. 224–225), Adolf Hitler has indicated the importance of this question as follows: "When I listened to Gottfried Feder's first lecture on breaking down the thraldom of interest in June, 1919, I knew at once that here we had a theoretic truth which will be of immense importance for the future of the German nation. . . . The *campaign against international loans and finance has become the chief point in the Programme for the German nation's struggle for independence and liberty.*"

All really serious National Socialists share this conviction, for fundamentally understood the solution of this question implies the rational solution of the Jewish question—and much more than that.

Antisemitism is in a sense the emotional foundation of our movement. Every National Socialist is an Antisemite, but not every Antisemite becomes a National Socialist. Antisemitism is purely negative; the Antisemite recognizes the carrier of the national plague-germ, but this knowledge is usually transformed into mere hatred of the individual Jew and the success of the Jews in business life. Antisemitism demands the expulsion of the Jew from our State and our economic life. The Antisemite does not worry his head about "How?" and "What next?"

If the spiritual foundations of the present Jewish supremacy: "Individual interest before the common interest," and its material means of power, the economic system of the Jewish bank, with its loans and credits, were still permitted to exist after the expulsion of the Jews, there would be enough Jewish bastards or "normal Germans" of miserable mongrel blood to take the place of the Jews; and they would rage against their own people no less furiously than do the heterodox Jews today—and we might even see "Antisemites" flocking to fill the places formerly filled by the Jews.

Now National Socialism, with its main demand, "Abolish the Thraldom of Interest," is essentially constructive. It bites deeper than mere Antisemitism, and the consequences are far more comprehensive.

In my essay, *Das Herzstück unseres Programms* (Nat. Soz. Jahrbuch, 1927), I pointed to the peculiar position that this demand gives us among all other Parties and Associations. As regards all our other demands, we find similar and parallel aspirations in the Parties of the Right and Left. No other Party than ours can show the counterpart of this one demand.

We all know that neither the Left, with their false cry of "Down with Capitalism," nor the Right, with their phrases about the Fatherland, are capable of initiating a new world epoch, for neither the Marxists nor the reactionaries could alter anything in the nature of our economy. They could only destroy, as the Communists in Russia have done. They are as incapable of construction as the Communists.

WHAT DO WE MEAN BY THE "THRALDOM OF INTEREST"?

The condition of the nations under the money-domination of Jewish high finance.

The landowner is subject to this thraldom who has to raise loans to finance his farming operations—loans at such high interest as almost to eat up the results of his labour—or who is forced to incur debts and to drag his mortgages after him like an everlasting leaden weight.

So is the worker, producing in shops and factories for a bare pittance, while the shareholder draws dividends and bonuses for which he has not worked.

So is the wage-earning middle class, which today is working almost entirely to pay the interest on bank credits.

So are all who have to earn their bread by mental or manual work, while a comparatively small proportion, without trouble or toil, pocket huge profits out of their dividends, Stock Exchange speculations, and financial transactions, etc. We do not refer to the thrifty savers and small capitalists—though they too owe, or did owe, their winnings to a false system—but throughout their lives many times the amount of their modest dividends was taken from them in the form of taxes, so that we can easily afford to repay them in their old age some part of the full earnings which were taken from them. I shall have more to say about this later on.

So is the industrialist, who has laboriously built up his business, and turned it in the course of time into a company. He is no longer a free agent, but has to satisfy the greedy board of directors, and the shareholders also, if he does not wish to be squeezed out.

So are all those nations that cover their deficits by means of loans.

This thraldom spells ruin for any nation that hands over to the money power, the bankers, its sovereign rights at home, the control of its finances, its railways, and its taxes and tariffs, as Germany has done by accepting the Dawes Plan

Creative labour is under the same thraldom, if it thinks of money before all else. Today money, the "servant of business," has become the master, and indeed the brutal tyrant of labour.

The thraldom of interest is the true expression for the antitheses: Capital *versus* Labour, Money *versus* Blood, Exploitation *versus* Creative Work.

The necessity of shattering this thraldom is of such vast importance for our nation and our race that on it alone depends the nation's hope of rising up out of its shame and slavery; the hope of restoring happiness, prosperity, and civilization throughout the world.

"It is the pivot on which everything turns; it is far more than a mere requirement of financial policy. While its principles and consequences bite deep into political and economic life, it is a leading problem of economics, profoundly affecting the personal life of the individual, and so demanding from one and all the decision: National service or unrestricted private enrichment. It means 'the solution of the Social Question.' "

All "world-problems" can be compressed into a word, which rises like a flaming signal out of chaos; yet a hundred prophets and a thousand books cannot exhaust all the questions which arise out of that word.

We can say no more at present on this vast basic principle of National Socialism. I have already thrown some light on every essential side of the problem in my pamphlets: *Das Manifest zur Brechung der Zinsknechtschaft*—Munich, 1926 (now out of print); *Der Staatsbankrott, Die Rettung*—Jos. C. Huber, Diessen, 1919; *Der kommende Steuerstreik*—Diessen, 1921, and *Der Deutsche Staat auf nationaler und sozialer Grundlage*—Frz. Eher Nachf., Munich (all obtainable through the library of our Party in Munich, Thierschstr. 11).

Intensive study is required to master the details of this problem, for the practical economics of the last fifty years have followed the capitalistic idea so closely that all who have grown up with it need a complete change of orientation in order to win free of it.

A pamphlet on the subject will shortly appear, which will give our members a full explanation of this most important task of the coming Nationalist State.

In addition to these two most important and novel basic principles of our Programme, we must mention certain others in connection with the economic, financial, social, cultural, and general policy of the State.

The principle underlying our policy of the State is simply this: *The German Reich is the home of the Germans.*

In this political principle is comprehended the whole vast domain of our foreign policy, including Germany's political liberation, with all the requirements of our racial policy, and the conditions and consequences of membership of the State.

Our economic principle is: *The task of the National economy is to provide the necessities of life, not to secure the highest possible rate of interest for capital.*

This principle of economic policy embraces a fundamental attitude of National Socialism to private property, to the building up of our economy in its various organized forms, from the very small to the very great —Syndicates and Trusts—and also to the great moral questions which must be a living force in economics, if "national economics" is not to degenerate into the exploitation of the nation and mere profit-making.

Our policy as regards finance is as follows:

Finance shall serve the State; the financial magnates shall not form a State within the State.

Here we have a principle which involves an overwhelming change. For the methods to be employed include the practical measures which will have to be taken to break the Thraldom of Interest—nationalization of finance, control of the credit and banking system.

Our principle as regards social policies is as follows:
The general welfare is the supreme law.

This principle of ours is in direct opposition to present-day practice, according to which every class, every profession, tries to win advantages for its own particular group in the social and political arena without regard to the general interest. We wish to make it possible for all to find a home and for all to make a living, and to institute a general system of care for the aged.

As regards educational and moral progress, it is our unchangeable principle: that all work in this direction is to be done from the sole standpoint of pure German nationality. The moral and intellectual forces of our nation may introduce a new Renaissance, a new classic age of all the fine arts, but they cannot do so to order, under compulsion, or with deliberate intention. On the other hand, the profound injury done to our German artistic and intellectual life at the hands of the Jewish dictatorship must be stopped by appropriate measures, especially by the disinfection of the Press.

Apart from this important domain of public life there are, of course, plenty of other improvements to be considered.

It is clear that the Law must evolve new concepts of public law to accord with innumerable innovations; that the scandal of the democratic Parliamentary vote will have to be removed, and that, following the transitional period of a Dictatorship, we shall have to decide on the outward and visible form of the State and the internal political structure of the provinces.

Already, however, we can see in this brief outline the general ordering of these questions in the light of the tremendous fundamental principles of our Programme.

It is not fundamental—in fact it is indifferent to us —whether we have a monarchy or a republic, whether we have a federation of five or twenty-five Federal States, or provinces, or tribal States, provided that all German States, combined under a strong central government, face the foreigner like a rock of bronze, and provided only that the citizens of the German State may live happy and contented in their home.

IV

THE REQUIREMENTS OF THE PROGRAMME IN DETAIL

AS FORMULATED BY GOTTFRIED FEDER IN
DER DEUTSCHE STAAT

It will make for clarity, when enlisting new members, to make use of the Programme in the form which follows. The minor clauses are ranged under the more important headings, corresponding to the principles enunciated in the preceding chapter.

THE POLITICAL AND ECONOMIC PROGRAMME OF THE N.S.D.A.P

Our aim is—Germany's re-birth in the German spirit to German liberty.

The means to this end are:

I. The political axiom: *The German Reich is the home of the Germans.*

(*a*) In foreign policy:

    1. Formation of a closed national State, embracing all of German race.

    2. Energetic representation of German interests abroad.

(*b*) In racial policy:

    3. Dismissal of all Jews and non-Germans from all responsible positions in public life.

    4. Prevention of immigration of Eastern Jews

and other parasitic foreigners. Undesirable foreigners and Jews may be deported.

(c) In internal policy:

5. None but Germans who profess entire community with the culture and destiny of Germany may exercise the rights of a citizen of the State.

6. He who is not a German may live in the German State only as a guest and subject to the Alien Laws.

7. The rights of Germans shall have the preference over those of citizens of foreign nations.

II. Our economic principle: *The duty of the State is to provide the necessaries of life and not to secure the highest possible rate of interest for capital.*

8. National Socialism recognizes private property on principle and gives it the protection of the State.

9. The National welfare, however, demands that a limit shall be set to the amassing of wealth in the hands of individuals.

10. All Germans form a working community for the promotion of the general welfare and culture.

11. Within the limits of the obligation of every German to work, and the fundamental recognition of private property, every German is free to earn his living and to dispose of the results of his labour.

12. The healthy combination of all forms of business, small and large, in every domain

E

of economic life, including agriculture, shall be encouraged.

13. All existing businesses which until now have been in the form of companies shall be nationalized.

14. Usury and profiteering and personal enrichment at the expense of and to the injury of the nation shall be punished with death.

15. Introduction of a year's obligation to work (for the State), incumbent on every German.

III. Our financial principle: *Finance shall exist for the benefit of the State; the financial magnates shall not form a State within the State.* Hence our aim to *abolish the thraldom of interest.*

16. Relief of the State, and hence of the nation, from its indebtedness to the great financial houses which lend money on interest.

17. Nationalization of the Reichsbank and the issuing houses.

18. Provision of money for all great public objects (water-power, communications, etc.), not by means of loans, but by granting non-interest bearing State bonds or without using ready money.

19. Introduction of a fixed standard of currency on a secured basis.

20. Creation of a communal building and agricultural bank (currency reform) for granting non-interest bearing loans.

21. Fundamental remodelling of the system of

taxation on social-economic principles. Relief of the consumer from the burden of indirect taxation, and of the producer from crippling taxation (fiscal reform and relief from taxation).

IV. Our social-political principle: *The general welfare is the supreme law.*

22. Development on a large scale of Old Age Insurance by nationalizing the system of annuities. Every necessitous member of the German State shall be assured of an adequate income on attaining a certain age, or, if permanently disabled, before that age.

23. Participation by all engaged in productive or value-creating enterprises in the revenues of the enterprise, all being jointly responsible for the fulfilment of the national economic obligations of the enterprise.

24. Seizure of all profits made out of the War and the Revolution not due to honest work, and of the fortunes of usurers and money-grabbers, and their application to the extension of social services.

25. Relief of the housing shortage by extensive fresh construction of dwelling-houses throughout the Reich by the means suggested in No. 20 (a new national building and agricultural bank).

V. Cultural policy: Our *highest cultural* aim is that *all the sciences and fine arts shall flourish on the basis of a politically free, economically healthy State.* The means of achieving this will be:

26. Training the young to become physically sound and intellectually free human beings, in accordance with the great traditions of German culture.
27. Complete liberty of creed and conscience.
28. Special protection for the Christian denominations.
29. Suppression and discouragement of dogmas which are opposed to the German moral sense and whose content is injurious to the State and the nation.
30. Suppression of all evil influences in the Press, in literature, on the stage, in the arts, and in the picture theatres.
31. Liberty of instruction in the German secondary schools; and the formation of a leading class of men of high character.

VI. Military affairs:

32. To make the nation efficient in defence by granting every free German the right to bear arms.
33. Abolition of mercenary troops.
34. Creation of a national Army for home defence under the command of a strictly disciplined corps of professional officers.

VII. Other reforms:

35. Press reform. Suppression of all printed matter which offends the dignity of the German people. Strict responsibility for all untruthful and intentionally distorted news.

36. Modification of the franchise so as to eliminate the demoralizing methods of electoral contests, and the irresponsibility (immunity) of those elected.

37. Formation of special Chambers for trades and professions.

38. Judicial reform as regards:

    the Land Laws—(recognition on principle of the rights of property in land; the owner may not borrow from private sources on the security of the land; the State to have the right of pre-emption, especially in the case of foreigners and Jews; the State to be empowered to administer estates in the event of bad management on the part of the owner).

    Civil Law—(greatly increased protection for personal honour and health, as opposed to the one-sided legal protection of the rights of property, which predominates at the present day).

39. Constitutional Reform.

    The *form of State* most suited to the German character is sovereign control concentrated in a supreme head. Whether this central power shall be wielded by an elected monarch or a president must be left to the decision of the nation.

    Federal character of the Reich.

    The constitution of the German nation, consisting as it does of a number of countries closely bound together by race and history, makes it necessary that each of the States shall enjoy the most comprehensive independence in internal affairs.

It is the function of the Reich to represent the German nation abroad, and to provide for passports and customs, also for the Army and Navy.

There are three main obstacles to carrying out this national Programme of National Socialism: Marxism, the Parliamentary system, and finance, which is superior to both.

1. Our anti-Marxist campaign is directed against the disruptive doctrine of the Jew, Karl Marx—against the doctrine of the class-war which splits up the nation—against the doctrine of the abolition of private property, which makes business impossible, and against the purely economic and materialistic view of history.

2. Our campaign against Parliament is directed against the irresponsibility of the so-called representatives of the people, who—enjoying immunity—can never be actually called to account for the results of their decisions; also against all the evils which arise out of the system (moral corruption, nepotism, venality), and the worst consequence of all—a Government which is dependent on such a Parliament.

3. Our campaign against Mammon, which ranks above the other two, is directed against the world-embracing power of finance, i.e. the perpetual exploitation of our nation by the great lending houses.

It is also a tremendous struggle against the soul-killing, materialistic spirit of greed and rapacity, with all its disruptive accompaniments, in all sections of our public, commercial, and cultural life.

The main battle is one between two world-philosophies, represented by two essentially different intellectual structures—the active and creative spirit and the labile, acquisitive spirit. The creative spirit, rooted to earth, yet overcoming the world in supersensual experience, finds its chief representative in the Aryan man; the acquisitive, rootless, commercial, materialistic spirit, aiming solely at worldly success, finds its chief representatives among the Jews.

National Socialism, like Antisemitism, regards the materialistic Jewish spirit as the chief cause of evil; it knows, however, that this greatest struggle in history must not stop short at merely negative Antisemitic demands; which is why the whole political and economic programme of National Socialism goes far beyond the theoretical or negative Antisemitic campaign, for it offers a creative and constructive picture, showing how the National Socialist State of labour and achievement must appear when completed.

Once this high aim is achieved the National Socialist Party will dissolve automatically; *for National Socialism will then have become the way of life of the whole German nation.* The N.S.D.A.P. is above all not a Parliamentary Party in the ordinary sense of the word, but is that section of the nation which is confident and sure of the future, which has gathered round strong and determined leaders to deliver Germany from shame and impotence abroad and from demoralization at home, and to make her once again strong and respected abroad, and morally and economically healthy at home.

The German Reich is the home of the Germans

Every word of this constitutional axiom is like the cut of a whip, when we consider the miserable state of things today.

The "German Reich"—where is there a German Reich today? Can the colony of Germany lay claim to the honourable name of a self-governing State? No! Not even the most complacent pundits of constitutional law could describe a country such as Germany is now as one in full enjoyment of its rights of sovereignty.

The five most important sovereign rights of a State are: sovereignty over its territory, over its army, over its finances, over its internal administration and communications, and lastly over its justice.

It is enough to put the matter thus to any layman, without further explanation of a nation's rights under International Law, and compare it with Germany's position today, and it becomes clear that it is impossible to maintain that a sovereign "German Reich" any longer exists.

Our territorial sovereignty is a mockery, for whenever France chooses she can occupy German soil without asking leave and without suffering opposition. Czechs, Poles, Danes can venture on any inroad into German territory without let or hindrance. The

"accursed old régime" put a very different interpretation on the slightest infringement of frontiers. A
military inroad into German territory then implied a
"state of war."

To protect its territorial sovereignty a nation needs
an armed force capable of repelling any inroad upon
the territory of the State, and therefore on the lives
and happiness of its nationals. A free State cannot
permit a foreign Power to scrutinize its actions, or to
have the right of deciding the strength, equipment,
armaments, and garrisons of its Army; if it does it
certainly is not "sovereign"; it cannot command its
means of power; it has given up control of its military
forces. Germany has done this by giving in to the
enemy Commissions for Disarmament and Control.

Germany had already suffered this humiliation by
accepting the Armistice conditions, and had lost her
sovereign international rights.

Nevertheless, she might have retained some part of
her internal sovereignty; but as soon as the military control was destroyed the financial magnates seized the opportunity for the limitless exploitation of German labour.

First of all the muddy torrent of Revolution burst
forth over Germany; then the usurers and profiteers,
the sons of chaos, Social-Democratic traitors, deserters,
and jail-birds, filled the highest and most lucrative
posts in the State, presently sharing their power with
the Democrats and Centre, and behind all and above
all the financiers, the Jews, got to work. Presently the
Freemasons of the so-called National Parties, espe-

cially Brother Stresemann, were called in. The final
blow was soon to come. The experts, with their Dawes
Plan, robbed Germany of the control of her finances,
which was bartered away to a handful of Jews, the
German and foreign financial magnates. The Reichstag
let the railways go, and with them all control of communications, and also a great part of the control of
taxation and customs, by handing them over to the
Reparations Commissioner.

We can hardly speak any longer of our judicial
sovereignty. The occupied districts are under foreign
military law; drastic exceptional laws govern the rest
of Germany, such as those for the defence of the
Republic. Insecurity of legal rights, organized robbery
of the nation through the so-called *Aufwertungsgesetze*,
forcing the Courts to declare that wrong is right.

Germany is no longer a sovereign State. She is a
colony of slaves. Germans are oppressed, thrown into
prison, denied free speech—simply because they are
still "German" and desire to end their slavery.

Yes, we want to have Germany free again, and this
coming German Reich shall be the home of the
Germans—not merely a machine for keeping order,
not merely a "State," an "authority," a "Government," a sinecure for a handful of reigning houses,
but a *Home*. Home—that sweet, magic word—the
love of home, intimate and beautiful, sunny, beloved.
The scent of our native soil rises in the nostrils; the
wanderer thrills with joy to feel the soil of home
beneath his feet; he is bound to it by ties of blood.

The feeling of security is the essence of the sense of home, and from that blossoms the fine flower of the love of home. The State and the nation can have no finer aim than this.

This is greater than a cautious social policy, than unemployment insurance, than housing schemes, though indeed the possession of a home of one's own is one of the strongest incentives to the love of home.

Home is more than an "Imperial Sovereign State," which one serves, perhaps out of enthusiasm, perhaps under compulsion.

Home is more than an Imperial or State or municipal administration, more than the representation of one's personal or professional interests, more than a manger, or the protection of person or property. All these public provisions must minister to the idea of the home. Just as in a properly constituted family the word "home" has a quite peculiar charm for the children, just as the words "at home" arouse quite other feelings than those evoked by the thought of a room in a hotel, although one may live in it, or a prison cell, so one's home is something unutterably sweet and yet mighty, far above the sordid idea of the expedient association to which the liberal, democratic, parliamentary conception of the structure of society gives the name of "State."

POLICY OF THE STATE

Principle: *The German Reich shall be the home of the Germans*—not of the Jews, Russians (Communists),

Social Democrats, who know no Fatherland called Germany (Crispien), nor of any foreigners who may make a longer or shorter stay on German soil.

We are in profound and fundamental opposition to the Weimar Constitution, which speaks only of "German nationals," but ignores the conception of "German" in the national, or more exactly, in the racial sense.

So each of the seven following theses is divided into three paragraphs, relating to (A) foreign policy, (B) population, (C) citizenship.

(A) Foreign Policy

1. *Creation of a closed national State, embracing all branches of the German race.*

It is the axiomatic right of every self-conscious nation that it should strive to include all the members of its race in a closed national State. This demand found spontaneous expression in the "Right of Self-Determination" proclaimed during the war by our enemies themselves.

Consequently we do not surrender a single German who lives beyond the frontiers of the German State and within the frontiers of another civilized State or colony, as regards his national membership with the German Reich. We should explain, however, that we have not any thought of wishing to effect the forcible absorption of Germans living outside Germany under Danish, Polish, Czech, Italian or French rule. We do, however, expect that our German brothers living under foreign Governments shall be accorded equal rights with the rest of the citizens in those countries.

This demand is therefore devoid of any Imperialistic tendency. It is the simple and natural demand that every powerful nationality asserts and recognizes as a matter of course.

2. *The vigorous representation of German interests abroad is a further and necessary corollary of Point 1.*

It is usually the best, most industrious and adventurous—engineers, explorers, professors, merchants, doctors—who go into the world, carrying German Kultur with them. They are members of the great German national family, to which they must never be lost. They have a right to expect protection from home when they are abroad. They should be not merely disseminators of Kultur, but the conscious advance-guard of the Germanic idea in the world; not "apostles of humanity," but bearers of the Nordic idea.

Those who represent Germany abroad must not try to "feel at home" in a foreign way of life, but the preservation of their German individuality, the superior German character, must be the task of Germans abroad, and of our official representatives. Our dusty Foreign Office must be swept clean with an iron broom. We have done with the obsequiousness towards the foreigner of our Erzbergers and Stresemanns, and it will be seen that the vigorous representation of German interests will be quite otherwise respected, and instead of kicks and slaps in the face, German desires will receive respect and consideration.

(B) RACIAL POLICY

3. *Exclusion of Jews and all non-Germans from all responsible positions in public life.*

This demand is so natural to us National Socialists that no further explanation is needed; but it is not possible to give brief and convincing arguments to those who fail to grasp the principles of our racial doctrine.

Anyone who sees in the Jews merely "German citizens of the Jewish religion"—and not an alien, sharply segregated people, strongly parasitic in character—will fail to appreciate the essential nature of this demand. If a man were to say or think that a cabbage which had grown by chance in the middle of of a strawberry bed was a strawberry plant, and that good strawberries could be got from it, he would be as wrong as if he thought that a lion cub which had got in among a flock of sheep had thereby become a sheep. A German would not do well as a judge or magistrate in China or India, and we should not like to have a Hottentot as a treasurer or Mayor of a German municipality.

And yet it would be better to have an Enver Pasha or a Chang Kai Chek reducing Germany to order than to give a Jew free play for his disintegrating racial characteristics. One thing is certain: that the Revolution loosened the bonds of order in the State, and that the long-established Jewish bankers, as well as the Jews from the East who have recently immigrated into Germany, have enriched themselves by impoverishing Germany. We have all seen and had experience of this; it has always been going on, this disintegration of the Nordic order. "There is but one way open for this crafty people—so long as *order* is maintained it has nothing to hope for." (Goethe at the fair at Plundersweilen.) Therefore we demand:

4. *That the immigration of Eastern Jews and other parasitic aliens shall be stopped, and that undesirable aliens and Jews shall be deported.*

At the time of the great inflation these Jews from Galicia and Poland flocked like vermin into the cities of Germany. Though there was a great dearth of houses they soon found the finest dwellings, while the Germans had to creep into holes. Then they started their dirty business, buying up everything—pearls, Persian carpets, diamonds, gold, silver, platinum, War Loan certificates, thousand-mark notes, copper, lead, literature, theatres, grain (the Evaporator Company). Very soon they were visibly rich, and took rank as Germans—in the eyes of "normal Germans."

Under National Socialist pressure the General Commissary of State, von Kahr, in Bavaria (the man who "broke his word of honour for reasons of State," who cravenly and treacherously allowed the German rising of November 9, 1923, to be stifled in blood), ventured one fine morning to agree to the expulsion of the Eastern Jews, and even sent his police gazette to a few of the most notorious speculators. Thereupon the "long-established" respectable Jews of the "Central

Association" interceded for their Galician vermin, for their Jewish "compatriots," and Kahr cravenly retreated.

Only perfectly lucid and unbending leaders of the State will deal with this matter, in accordance with their anthropological knowledge. No compromise can be permitted here.

Over and above this purely Antisemitic application of it, racial hygiene must be fostered, and the lofty aim—*the supreme aim of the Nordicizing of our people in the spirit of the Nordic ideal*—must be promoted.

Perhaps this question is not properly included in the "time programme" of the N.S.D.A.P., but we must all clearly realize that nothing very permanent can be achieved with the so profoundly bastardized German people.

But we can already assert that the terrible racial ebb has been stemmed for the time—at all events in theory—merely by the fact of the extraordinary interest which racial problems and racial literature have aroused in a large circle of readers, and by the fact that fundamental works on these subjects do exist; but only indefatigable effort will achieve any real progress.

(c) As regards State Citizenship we Demand:

5. *That none but Germans who believe in German "Kultur" and the common destiny of all Germans shall enjoy the rights of a citizen of the State.*

Even here limits must be drawn. People who, even though German-born, act consciously in a way injurious to the nation and the State, and receive and obey orders from abroad, do not belong to the German community of destiny, and therefore cannot exercise the rights of citizenship, any more than a Jew can do so, and there are many to whom we shall have to deny the high honour of enjoying these rights.

6. *Non-Germans may dwell in the German State only as guests, and shall be subject to the Alien Laws.*

This is a necessary principle, calculated to put an end forever to the eternal obsequiousness towards every foreigner. But it does not mean that we shall not welcome citizens of a foreign country warmly, and treat them well as guests, so long as they conduct themselves properly; but

7. *The rights and interests of Germans shall have precedence over those of the subjects of a foreign nation.*

Further details of our requirements need not be included in our Programme. For instance, precise details of the "Alien Laws" can be settled later, and also the methods for the expulsion of the Jews. One cannot demand of a programme of fundamental principles that it shall also be a programme of action, giving tactical details for the attainment of political power, or for special tasks. I am, for that matter, opposed to an immediate preoccupation with programmes, for in our terrific struggle we are concerned primarily with an irrevocable statement of our aims, not with the preparation of "electoral" or other programmes such as the bourgeois or Socialist parties publish.

F

ECONOMIC POLICY

It is the duty of the National Government to provide the necessaries of life and not to secure the highest possible dividends for Capital.

To the straightforward mind of the simple man it might seem superfluous to emphasize such an obvious truth in a special and even systematic fashion. The productive worker—the farmer, the manual labourer, the artisan, the manufacturer, or the worker employed in one of the many subsidiary trades concerned in the carriage or distribution of goods—knows, so to speak, by instinct that what he produces is used or consumed: consumed by himself, or used as a means of exchange for other goods.

In his eyes "business" which is not concerned with production or consumption is ridiculous, impossible, nonsensical.

This brings us to one of the great intellectual difficulties in our recruiting work. We are obliged to tell our fellow-countrymen: Your natural feeling is of course perfectly correct as regards the meaning and purpose of work and the national economy, but unfortunately our so-called economy of today does not in any way respond to this natural demand. If you look closer you will on the contrary discover the most alarming features, which are utterly opposed to the obvious duty of the national economy.

For what are the usurers and profiteers doing? Do these universal plunderers give a thought to providing the necessaries of life? No! Are they engaged in creating values; do they produce anything? No! They are robbers and traitors in the economic sense, and merely amass wealth for themselves.

What are the banks doing? They circulate money and give "credit." Yes; but the Post Office does this, and more cheaply, and quickly, and better; and to whom do the banks give credit?—To the needy, the labouring masses, who have no home of their own, or for building houses, for supplying the crying need of dwellings? No! Or to the farmers, or the manufacturers, or the business men who produce and distribute the economic necessaries? Rarely, and only if the borrower can offer security over and above the natural engagement to repay, and is prepared to pay a special rate of interest. Do the banks care whether the producers' customers are served well, cheaply and promptly, or whether economic necessaries are supplied quickly, cheaply, and with due attention? No! Their one thought is to make their profit out of their interest, commission, or whatever the banks' process of tapping the supply of money is called. What do the banks produce? Nothing! What do they earn? Vast sums.

Thus money-lenders, profiteers, bankers, financiers, supply no sort of *need*, yet they derive huge profits from the prevailing capitalist system: in fact, they tyrannize over and exploit the anti-social economic system. Today the main function of commerce is to ensure the "rentability" of borrowed capital; that is, under our system of usurious capitalism the workers have at present to surrender a good proportion of their earnings to the great capitalists of the banks and stock exchanges, and to international usurers and speculators. What does the "employer" do, to give him his usual name—or the "bloodsucker," the "exploiter," as the workers call him? He endeavours, by paying the lowest possible wages, by using inferior material, by mass production or "costing" on the one hand, and by charging the highest prices on the other hand, to squeeze out the highest possible profits for his own pocket.

He gives no thought to his employees' poverty; it is all one to him if his wares have soon to be thrown away as rubbish—all the better, since this means more work and more profits for him. The people are always foolish enough to buy more cheap rubbish if it is enticingly recommended and displayed. Here we see the cancerous evil of the great stores.

His main concern is his "profit," the "rentability" of his capital; the "supply of necessaries" is only a means to an end.

But after all, he does do something—he creates employment.

The true employer, he who is conscious of his high task as an economic leader, is a very different person. He must be a man of moral worth—in the economic sense at least. His task is to discover the real economic needs of the people—if he is also an inventor he does this pioneer work himself. He must keep his costs as low as he can, and lay them out to the best advantage; must keep prices as low as possible in order to get his goods on to the market; must maintain both the quality and quantity of his output, and must pay his employees well, so that they may be able to purchase goods freely; and he must always be thinking of improvements of his plant and his methods of trading. If he puts these things first in his business, he is "supplying the necessaries of life" in the best and highest sense, and his profits will come of themselves without his making them his first object. The finest and most universally known example of this kind of manufacturer is Henry Ford. There are other names in our own heavy industries which stand equally high —Krupp, Kirdorf, Abbe, Mannesmann, Siemens, and many more.

The character of such businesses is altogether different when they are not personally controlled by men of high moral qualities, who look after the interests of their workers, but are handed over to impersonal limited companies.

So long as the founder of such a business, as the chief shareholder, can maintain the sterling traditions of his establishment, all may be well; but, as a general thing, soon after the business is converted it is overwhelmed by the shareholders' demands for profits— that is, by the demands of the capitalist moneylenders. The former owners, the managers, now depend on the

Board, representing the shareholders, for improvements in business methods and working conditions, and the shareholders have no interest (beyond that of the slave-driver) in the welfare of the workers and the quality of their work, so long as they can draw high dividends on their invested capital. The introduction of bearer stock has had a most devastating influence, for any chance speculator can corner the shares, and actually become the owner of large industrial works without knowing anything about them. To the men of the Stock Exchange stocks and shares are merely so much paper for them to play with. They are not interested in conditions of production and labour; most of them could not say what products or conditions of marketing, labour, wages, and maintenance obtain in the business of which they are the legal owners (!). And owners they are, just because they happen to have cornered the shares of this or that factory in the market.

Let us now examine this state of affairs in the light of its effect on the national economy, so that we may realize the corrupt character of the capitalist system.

Today business looks merely for profit, for dividends.

The large retail stores, all in the hands of Jews—Tietz, Wertheim, Karstadt, etc., etc.—follow a somewhat different method, to which I have already alluded. They depend on "charm," "display," "bluff," and the awakening of wholly unnecessary "demands" for "luxuries."

Great palaces, of enormous proportions, built with all the refinements of art, invite the public to purchase apparently cheap, but for the most part quite useless, articles, and by offering easy conditions of payment they entice their customers to spend all manner of sums on pure luxuries. Rest-rooms are provided to enable people to spend a long time in the stores, which thus become mere hotbeds of extravagance, for let no one imagine that he gets anything as a present. Really prosperous people don't buy in large stores; they know what the poorer ones don't know—he who buys cheap buys dear. Do the crowds who buy in those palaces imagine that they were built otherwise than with their saved-up pennies? Do they think they can escape paying for the escalators, the lifts, the rest-rooms, the fairy-like illumination?

Realize, also, that the large stores spell ruin to the small shop-keepers, that they exploit home labour and their staffs most cruelly, that what is manufactured for them is mostly rubbish. The better articles are usually dearer than in the respectable specialized shops, a fact which justifies our fight against the large stores. We regard them as a special form of the capitalistic idea in practical operation, which does not provide necessaries of life, but exists merely for the purpose of producing huge profits for the shareholders.

After this primary standpoint of providing the necessaries of life (which, we should observe, has nothing to do with the Communist scheme of economic planning), the question that ranks first in importance is our attitude towards private property.

8. *National Socialism recognizes private property on principle and places it under the protection of the State*—provided that it is acquired and employed honourably. We cannot discuss the matter exhaustively in these pages; but any one who rightly comprehends "work" cannot for a moment doubt that the product of "work" must be the property of him who works. A producer will fail to understand why his work, or its value, should be the property of a vague "community," nor will he readily admit that the fruits of his labour should go to an individual, the capitalist. *Hence a right understanding of the meaning of "work" leads naturally to the recognition of private ownership.*

And lastly, we must speak of ultimate things—such as the ideal of the home. The Home is not a reality unless it stand on a man's own property, and shelters his own family. A man's own fruit and vegetables, out of his own garden, taste better than a meal eaten in a crowded eating-house. He who does not know the longing for possession or the joy of possession will fail to understand the importance of recognizing private ownership. Such a man is either an uprooted "city man," or a rootless "capitalist," who regards the property of the creative man as his booty, and understands the secret of acquiring the property of others by the methods of the capitalist usurer. It is characteristic of the predatory capitalist that he invariably has an insatiable appetite for more possessions—if possible, moveable property—while the Nordic man, the solid man of the soil, is absolutely modest in his ideas. He wants no more than he can earn by his work. A workman does not want a fine villa which he could never earn; he wants a nice little house of his own; not a hired one, for which, in the course of his life, he would be paying three or four times as much as the house cost to build. But the predatory Jew, the capitalist, does not want to be tied to any plot of land; his ideal is a big safe stuffed with scrip, mortgage deeds, and promissory notes. Wealth, not in possessions, but in other people's mortgaged property, is his aim. He does not work, but he never rests until he has acquired a sufficient number of debts or mortgages to give him the whip hand over his "debtors"—who really owe him nothing. The next demand of our Programme is framed in order to put a stop to this.

9. *The welfare of the nation demands that a limit shall be set to the immoderate amassing of wealth in the hands of individuals.*

Wealth and property are not injurious in themselves; on the contrary, a property well administered benefits all who work upon it. Once more, it is the capitalist system of loans which has turned wealth from a blessing into a curse; it is robbery and exploitation. The great mass of the propertyless workers and the indebted middle classes are becoming more and more sharply and harshly separated from the rich, from the capitalists; countless small owners have been distrained upon for debt and dispossessed, and the power of the financiers, who know no fatherland, no home-land, is becoming ever more sinister, as they sit in their modern robber-baron castles, the banks, and plunder the people. To meet this danger, in the National State:

10. *All Germans shall form a working community for the furtherance of the common welfare and culture.*

This idea of the community of work implies the economic overthrow of the universalist conception of society. All work and production must be comprised within the higher ideal of service to the community. This is in no way opposed to personal effort and industry, but it means that individual progress shall not be effected at the expense of one's fellows. No. 11 gives expression to this demand:

11. *Within the limits of the general duty to work incumbent on every German, and subject to the recognition of the principle of private ownership, every German shall be free to earn his living in whatever manner he chooses, and free to dispose of the results of his labour.*

The foregoing expressly rejects the Marxist "planned economy," as well as the socializing efforts of big capital. The State shall include the greatest possible number of free existences, linked by the social idea of service. It is, of course, out of the question to run mines, blast-furnaces, rolling-mills, or ship-yards on a small scale, but a hundred thousand free and independent master-shoemakers are better than five monster shoe factories.

The great landed estates in the North and East of Germany are more productive, being run on a large scale, than if managed by small freehold farmers. Small freeholds do best within easy reach of towns and villages. Our No. 12 demands that:

12. *A healthy combination of small, medium-sized, and large concerns, in all departments of economic life, including farming, shall be maintained.*

13. *Big business* (syndicates, trusts) *will be nationalized.*

This demand is consistent with our general war upon the capitalist idea.—The first aim of syndicates and trusts in any particular branch of production is to unite with other similar businesses for the purpose of dictating prices. They are governed by no desire to distribute good wares at a cheap price. Such "rings" are specially attracted by new businesses which are doing well. New firms in the same line of business are bought up and put out of the way, often at a very high cost by way of compensation. Supply is regulated by pooling, by which means they are able to regulate prices in accordance with an apparently genuine "supply and demand." This is what interests the shareholders, who have no desire to see prices kept low by competition. New ideas and inventions are viewed with a hostile eye, and preferably suppressed if their adoption would endanger the paying capacity of older plants. Such businesses, run as huge trusts from a big central office, are clearly "ripe for socialization," i.e., they have ceased to fulfil any of the services to the community which individual competition performs. They are by hypothesis stereotyped, and only serve the greed of capitalism.

14. *Usury and profiteering, and ruthless self-enrichment at the expense of the nation, shall be punished with death.*

The Law, as it is now, gives special protection to individual property. A petty theft, if not a first offence, is often punished inhumanely, whereas the Law affords no means of catching wholesale swindlers, who rob an entire nation by "capitalistic methods." We refer especially to those who promoted and profited by the inflation. It was the first time in history that a whole industrious nation was robbed of all its savings by a crime of inflation on the vast scale of the German devaluation of currency.

The greed of the banks after the stabilization was worse than highway robbery. More Germans fell victims to the practices of the "war companies" than to any organized band of robbers.

When the time comes we shall deal with these things in further detail, and shall have to find a legal formula for them. But everyone will agree that "organized fraud against the nation" must be punished as severely as, and even more so than, small individual thefts of money, or cases of individual fraud.

15. *Introduction of an obligatory year of labour (or service) for every German.*

The obligation to work will be the visible expression of the high ideal of serving the community. It is intended to be educational in effect, and to set before each German an example of the whole community working together as one man. In the strict fulfilment of duty it will show to every German the blessing of working for the service of the nation.

A special inquiry (in this series of pamphlets) will concern itself more fully with this problem.

FINANCIAL POLICY

Abolishing the Thraldom of Interest

Our opinions concerning this important subject have been so fully expounded in the second chapter, that we shall describe here only the measures suitable for achieving our objective in practice.

16. *Liberation of the State, and so of the nation, from its indebtedness (obligation to pay interest) to the great financial houses.*

The State may make no debts—for it has no need to do so. There is no comparison between the State and the private person who every now and then requires a loan and is forced to make debts. The State controls the Mint; it can thus *make money*, which the private person cannot do! It did this in a lunatic fashion during the inflation. It did the same with the Rentenmark, and the same—after resigning its control to the so-called Reichsbank—with the so-called Reichsmark.

The State could make far better use of this right to make money, without incurring the danger of inflation. But only if first:

17. *The Reichsbank and all the issuing banks are nationalized.*

18. *If funds are provided for all great public objects (water-power, railroads, etc.), not by means of loans, but by granting non-interest-bearing State bonds, or without using ready money.*

In other words:—The irresponsible printing of bank notes, without creating new values, means inflation. We have all lived through it. But the correct conclusion is that an issue of non-interest-bearing bonds by the State cannot produce inflation if new values are at the same time created.

The fact that today great economic enterprises cannot be set on foot without recourse to loans is sheer lunacy. Here a reasonable exercise of the State's right to create money might produce the most beneficial results.

It must be clear to anyone that—for instance—a great hydro-electric plant might be erected in the following unexceptionable manner:

The Government introduces a Bill in the Legislature for exploiting the water-power of Bavaria, Saxony, etc., due regard being given to all economic requirements. The local Diet, or other body, decides on the construction, and empowers the Finance Minister or the State Bank to issue a series of bank notes, marked specially to show that they are fully covered by the new works under contemplation. These notes are covered by the combined credit of the State and the Reich. No one can make any objection on the score of inflation.

Construction is carried out on the additional credit granted by the Council representing the nation, and the notes become legal tender like the rest.

When the work is completed, nitrates or electricity are supplied to customers against this money, and in a few years the issue can be recalled and destroyed. Result: The State, the nation, has instituted a new work, which secures to it a great new source of revenue, and the nation is the richer by it.

To prove the folly of the present system let us compare the foregoing with what occurs now:

A loan is taken up. A few capitalists do what the whole nation, even though Parliament may vote in favour of it, cannot do: they allow the State to borrow money from them. Instead of using its direct authority for the benefit of the nation, the State engages to pay permanent interest for the sum required to complete certain work, thereby hanging a mill-stone round its neck. And, what is most costly of all, it issues bonds, thus creating "fresh purchasing capacity." On the balance-sheet it makes no difference whether the new work is represented by new paper money or by new bonds. But the community suffers injury, because the bonds imply that the new work is mortgaged to capital, which naturally makes itself perfectly secure, dictates prices, and takes the profits. Thus it is really the financiers who are the richer by the development of the nation's water-power; they are indifferent as to repayment; they like to have such monopolies as permanent milch-cows. The people are forced to pay dearly for electric current or nitrates, and once again a part of the national property is converted to the interests of the financiers.

I must refer the reader to my earlier writings, especially *Der deutsche Staat*, which treats these questions in more detail than is possible in this pamphlet. Several numbers in this series, moreover, deal with various special aspects of the coming State's novel methods of creating money.

Point 19 demands the *introduction of a fixed standard of currency*. That we have now, of course, but the robbery is the same as of old. We National Socialists had everything ready, once we were in power, for making an end of the inflation swindle forthwith, and for introducing a new guaranteed standard of currency.

20. *Establishment of a new Building and Agricultural Bank for the benefit of the community.*

This demand is exhaustively explained in Pamphlet 8 of the National Socialist Library: *Die Wohnungsnot und die Sociale Bau-und Wirtschaftsbank als Retterin aus Wohnungselend, Wirtschaftskrise und Erwerblosene-lend*. It is worth noting that with this demand of ours for a financial policy we have penetrated deeply into other political circles besides our own.

In 1921 I submitted this demand to the Bavarian Government in the form of a fully elaborated Bill. There was at first much sympathy with the idea: but once the "experts"—the banking fraternity— were drawn into consultation, the Government rejected "Feder's Utopia."

After the successful Election in Thuringia in February 1924, our Party in the Landtag worked hard to establish such a bank, and found von Klüchtzner, the Finance Minister, prepared to co-operate; the bourgeois section also were in sympathy. By a majority vote in the Landtag the Government were empowered to establish a Social Bank for Building and Agriculture. Whereupon the Government of the Reich, *under pressure from the Reichsbank,* forbade the execution of the "popular will."

I had in the meanwhile contrived to have a draft Bill introduced in the Reichstag, providing for similar banks in the different States; in the short session of the Dawes year (1924), however, it was cautiously postponed by the Government parties until the dissolution in the autumn of that year.

A Bill for such a bank was laid before the Landtag of Mecklenburg. The Resolution was made ineffective by the vacillation of the German-Nationalist Finance Minister, in view of the obstacles which the Reichsbank was expected to place in its way.

The idea underlying such a Bank is as simple as the plan explained above for creating money for great public purposes.

A combined economic corporation, the so-called Building and Agricultural Bank, would be given the right to issue money for housing developments (*Baumark-Scheinen*) covered by the value of the newly-built houses. These could then be erected free from the huge burden of interest which alone today

G

makes it impossible to build houses in sufficient numbers.

Every German with a home of his own!

A free people on freehold soil!

21. *Complete remodelling of the system of taxation on social and national economic principles. Delivery of the consumer from the burden of indirect taxation and the producer from taxes which cramp his activities.* (Reform of and relief from taxation.)

I must refrain from giving details of these reforms here, as they will be given in a volume shortly to be published in the Nat. Soz. Library.

SOCIAL POLICY

Social policy is apparently the favourite slogan of our present political cure-alls. It sounds so nice, it makes them popular, and it attracts votes for the Party which promises to set everything right.

When every Party promises the official, for instance, an increase of pay, this is called Social Policy

It is the same when they promise to grant the wishes of the clerks and workers; or when they do a little to relieve the people with small incomes, or the war sufferers, or young teachers, or Germans abroad.

And the whole nation runs after these political rat-catchers when they play on their "social-policy" flute.

It must first be clearly understood that Social Policy denotes: *The public welfare the highest law;* and that, as now understood, Social Policy is really a policy of self-interest, having no regard for the general welfare. All sorts of careless promises are made, and those who make them must know from the outset that it is impossible to fulfil them.

Now that Germany is so powerless, politically, economically, and financially—an impotence which has found international expression first in the Dawes Laws, and now in the Young Law, and in the so-called policy of fulfilment, which has laid burdens on our nation that make life almost impossible—it is both false and ridiculous to talk of "Social Policy." Now that the German people are so cramped for room, when each man is treading on his neighbour and trying to get ahead of him and to push him aside, to play one class against another, and to promise to favour one group at the expense of the rest, is not "Social Policy for the general good" but a policy of inciting class against class. We know very well that a momentary "improvement" is annulled by a higher cost of living and higher taxation.

Social policy means something very different—a determination to solve the social problem.

The disinherited, the people "down on their luck" or deprived of social rights, the exploited working classes, believe that their just wages and their proper position in the social order are being withheld from them—hence the *class war*.

And who can deny that profound injuries, bitter injustice, have bitten deep into our economic life? Yet the conclusions drawn by Marxism, with its "class war" and its "social and economic demands" of "expropriating the expropriator," and "socialization," are utterly false, for they strike at all the true requirements of a genuine social policy, whose highest law is the general welfare.

Class war as a political principle—this is to preach *hatred* as a guiding principle. "Expropriation of the expropriator" makes *envy* a principle of economics, and "socialization" means striking down personality and leadership, and setting up material, the mass, in the place of interest and efficiency.

Today we need no other proof of the breakdown of the Marxist doctrines than the complete bankruptcy of the Communist system of economics and the miserable failure of the German Revolution of 1918.

I would call my readers' particular attention to the fact that this pseudo-socialism, born of Marxism, is not founded on common sense, nor on any "social" idea, and is not constructive, but is sunk in the lowest depths of political thought; that it is based on the crass individualism and the chaotic structure of society which have already been exposed in the first part of this pamphlet. We see only a multitude of individuals, bound together merely by hatred and envy—not intellectually and organically by a high ideal—at war upon the other half of the nation. Can we be surprised that the social question is not, and cannot be, solved by this means, and that the sole response is hatred and the desire for loot? No living State could result from the Marxist Stock Exchange revolt, but only a heap of ruins.

Once again National Socialism finds the right word: Stock Exchange revolt. Marxism is an obvious capitalistic bogey. Capitalistic, because when a society founded on individualism has fallen into chaos, it falls of necessity under the sway of the great financial magnates.

The "anti-capitalistic" social-political theories (Marxism, the class war)—that is, social policies as understood today—are necessarily capitalistic, for they are based on the same intellectual principle. They are not inspired by the wish to construct an organic, articulate order, to amalgamate, carefully and considerately, the various industrial classes under the high conception of national unity; their aspirations are purely selfish, and their wish is to better their own position without regard for others.

Capitalism and Marxism are one! They grow on the same intellectual base. There is a whole world of difference between them and us, their bitterest opponents. Our whole conception of the construction of society differs from theirs. It is neither a class-struggle nor class-selfishness; our supreme law is the general welfare

22. *Generous development of Old Age Insurance by nationalizing life-annuities. Every member of the German nation shall be assured of an adequate income on attaining a certain age, and before that age if permanently disabled.*

That is the solution of the social problem.

It is not so much direct discontent with wages,

salaries, and incomes that causes social tension, as uncertainty, insecurity, a man's anxiety as to his later years, the fear lest he may be flung on to the streets. It is this gnawing anxiety which drives the various occupations to join together in sham-social organizations of the Marxist and capitalist types, and embitters the struggle between employer and employee. It releases the basest instincts on both sides, and mutual animosity is the result. The worker's proper aim in life is lost sight of in the struggle for a temporary increase of wages, and he never achieves *the* great aim of social policy—*proper provision for old age.*

We note once again that the State arrived at a good and commendable solution in the case of the official class, by providing for them after retirement. It is the proper and happy solution of the capitalistic ideal of income, namely, to convert it into the *true* State's ideal of provision for its citizens, based on personal labour and efficiency.

It will be the highest and noblest aim of National Socialism to realize this standard of general welfare.

23. *Profit-sharing for all.*

The N.S.D.A.P. identifies itself with this demand. It is in fact a purely Socialistic demand in the proper sense of the word; nevertheless, it comes to us as an attractive but corrupting present from capitalism.

The sharing of profits arising out of the work of others is the kind of unearned income which is most sharply attacked by National Socialism. The sharing of the profits derived from a man's own work is a demand so natural, and socially so just, that nothing can be advanced against it as a principle.

It is in the execution of it that the difficulty arises: that is, in limiting the amount of the share due to the production, skill, and industry of the worker, and that due to the brain-work of the inventor, the accountant, the merchant, the manager, and circumstances connected with the business.

The demand for profit-sharing is of course of great importance as regards the productive wealth of the nation. Even under the present system some part of the booty which invested capital hopes to get out of a business might be recovered for the worker.

We will not discuss here the question of how, later on, the National Socialist State will solve the problem of profit-sharing.

I personally have held that to effect a general lowering of prices, at the same time maintaining wages at the present level, would be the better and more practical way to fulfil the demand for sharing the profits of the whole of our national production.

It is, however, possible that the National Socialist State will solve the problem in a far more comprehensive manner than is conceived today by minds with a Marxist and capitalistic orientation. The present demand for profit-sharing springs either from the desire for gain (essentially capitalistic) or from envy (essentially Marxist).

Only in the ideal sense, as National Socialism conceives it, is it justified, because, when we come to solve it, we must avoid the capitalistic method of granting a small share in the business, the sole object of which is to secure for the larger shareholders their right to their dividends, and also the Marxist idea of envy, for that debases the personality and injures the community.

We give a few examples for the sake of clarity.

It does no good to the "profit-sharing" workers in a shoe factory to get a few shares in the business, or a small bonus, or a pair of shoes at cost price, if they have to pay just as dearly for their shirts, suits, socks, food, and drink, because the tailors, butchers, bakers, and brewers cover the greed of the clothiers, bakeries, meat purveyors, and breweries by their own "profit-sharing."

The lowering of prices is the magic formula which must give every member of the nation a share in the profits of national production.

It will not satisfy the sense of social justice of the genuine National Socialist if the street-sweepers, stone-breakers, day-labourers, railway-men, postmen, transport-workers, dustmen, hospital-workers — to name only a few groups—are *permanently*, and agricultural labourers, miners, builders' labourers, almost always, excluded from profit-sharing, simply because these classes do not contribute to increase values. As regards agriculture (in which connection we must not consider merely the few large estates with farms, herds of cattle, forests, fish-ponds, etc., but also the millions of small- and medium-sized farms), we can only say that it "pays" in years when the harvest is good; and in the heavy industries even the mines yield only a bare profit under the pressure of world competition.

Can we say that these millions of workers and employees, who are often engaged in most important branches of industry, but who, owing to circumstances, can seldom or never hope for a direct share in profits, are to receive less consideration than the less numerous class who work, perhaps, as washers-up, or porters in a night-club, or a Turkish bath, or in an optical or chemical factory possessing a monopoly and enjoying an international reputation? Are the latter to share the profits and dividends on luxury production—are they to make it more and more impossible for the majority of the nation to enjoy these advantages?

We may of course recollect the shower of dividends, bonuses, and Christmas presents of money poured out upon workers, clerks, and officials who by years of work and special services have deserved well of their employers. Such efforts of a social-political nature need not be discussed or criticized in this treatise on general principles. The demand, as things are now, is an important demand, and one which attracts much attention. "Profits" depend mainly on the general business situation, and on the technical skill and salesmanship of the management; failure may come through faulty construction or a mistake in calculations. However skilled the workers may be, however industrious, they can exert little or no influence on the results of the year's work or on the gains or losses. Their efficiency justifies them in demanding a proper and sufficient wage, but there are no moral or economic grounds for their claiming a share in the profits. They would quite rightly resist the suggestion that they should cover any losses of the business year out of their savings; they would rightly protest against being expected to make up, by a lowering of wages, for bad management or extravagant living on the part of the directors. But "profit-sharing" is justifiable only if there is ability and readiness to share risks and losses, or if special efficiency merits it.

The immoderate accumulation of profits, in particular by concerns of a monopolistic nature within the national economy, is to be opposed on principle. The establishment of an ascendancy by means of the concentration of capital may constitute a danger when the capital is not administered in accordance with the National Socialist spirit. It will be necessary to inquire in each individual case how far such profits are in the public interest, and whether by reducing the prices of the goods placed on the market by such concerns the profits hitherto retained by them should not to some extent be passed on to the community.

24. *Expropriation of all profits not made by honest work, but through the war and the Revolution—and further, money gained by the stabilization and revaluation of the mark; also the property of misers and usurers.*

This is a measure of punishment and justice, requiring no explanation under any principle.

25. *Solution of the housing problem by extensive building throughout the Reich with the means provided under No. 20 (the Building and Agricultural Bank).* This closes the list of social-political demands. As to the technical, monetary, and economic problems, little can be said in this pamphlet, for this is a vast special subject, and one which, it would seem, only minds infected by capitalism can understand, and which will actually have to be tackled by them. Pamphlet 8 of the National Socialist Library deals fully with the subject.

CULTURAL POLICY

It is not possible, in a programme, to state more than a few leading principles. This has already been done. For the rest, it must be our principle not to drag "religious" questions into general political statements of our cultural policy. Only those who have completely mastered, for example, the Jewish problem, can make the secret doctrine of Judaism a subject of public exposition or attack. The example of such a high authority as Th. Fritsch shows us that even this distinguished Talmudic expert could not save himself from a sentence of several months' imprisonment. This does not mean that such a subject should be avoided, but only that these problems must be studied with the greatest thoroughness.

The same may be said of all the coarse, stupid attacks on Christianity. Expressions such as "Christianity has only done harm" merely show that the man who utters them has neither human nor political intelligence.

One may indeed blame the Church for meddling in politics, and all good Christians will disapprove of the cruelties practised in the name of the Cross by the Inquisition, and of the trials for witchcraft, but it is wrong to abuse in general terms the greatest phenomenon in human history because of the perversities and erroneous ideas and faults of individuals. The Christian religion has uplifted and strengthened millions upon millions, and brought them to God by the way of suffering.

The culture of the Middle Ages stands in the sign of the Cross; great achievements, self-sacrifice, and courageous faith had their roots in Christianity. Thus we must be careful to distinguish the inner spiritual kernel of Christianity from the various excrescences which have appeared upon it in its passage through history.

Our Party as such takes its stand upon the basis of positive Christianity.

This is not the place to discuss all the problems, all the hopes and desires as to whether the German nation may at some time discover some new form for its religious beliefs and experiences; these are matters of secular importance which surpass the scope of even such a revolutionary Programme as that of National Socialism.

It is of urgent importance to set our face against all the disruptive influences which are poisoning our people in the domain of art, literature, science, the stage, the moving pictures, and above all, throughout the entire Press. Our fundamental Programme —the 25 Points—is so detailed that I need not say more on this subject.

MILITARY AND OTHER REFORMS

The national Army, the Chambers of the trades and professions, reforms of the franchise and the law, are problems and provinces of public life so comprehensive that they cannot be dismissed in a few sentences. The leading ideas are set out in the Programme itself, but the task of thinking and working them out and, above all, of grafting them on to the historical past, will be the great problem of the coming years, when we hope that political power will be ours, and when it must find us equipped to deal as experts with the business of the State.

Here we have a rich field for research under National Socialism; and here again the surpassing greatness of the National Socialist ideal will be manifested.

The significance of National Socialism is shown precisely by the fact that it leaves no domain of the national life untouched; for it provides an entirely new foundation on which we shall have to build up that life.

WHAT WE DO NOT DESIRE

In order to strengthen the positive side of our Programme it will be well to state shortly what we *do not* desire.

We do not desire to turn the wheels of history backwards, nor to restore to life dynasties which have faded away, leaving hardly a trace of themselves— through their own fault. Nor do we desire to restore the classes that have been dethroned to their former privileged positions. The officer class and the officials are really no higher or better than any other professional classes, in so far as these genuinely serve the nation first and foremost, in the spirit of our ideal.

It is not uniform or gold lace, but performance, which makes the man.

We do not desire any one-sided preference or artificial elevation for the working class, nor any kind of proletarian dictatorship. Let no man talk himself into believing that any class may, simply because it has been oppressed in the past, assume a claim to be given power. Such aspirations, when translated into realities, infallibly lead to terrible consequences, such as those which accompanied the Stock Exchange revolt of November 1918. So far it is not the "oppressed" section of the population which is on top, but a crowd of political swindlers, greedy adventurers, profiteers, jabberers, and fools, who have got possession of the political machine and the administration. The promised dictatorship of the proletariat has turned into

The dictatorship of the "Profitariat"

Even a new ordering of the State under National Socialism could have no hope of success unless it had at its disposal a very thoroughly trained staff of resolute men completely imbued with the principles of our Programme; serious men of energy and experience. Even with us only too many mere demagogues would elbow their way upwards and reap advantage from the new order.

It is much easier to criticize the faults of a collapsing social order than to do constructive work on it.

We require not merely a new Party, slowly obtaining a footing in Parliament and the administration, and then perhaps accepting a post or two in a coalition Ministry, only to get its back broken in the end—for then our part in history would be played, just as today Social Democracy is finished as a political and intellectual force in Germany. The same thing applies to the German Nationalists, who have already gone back on their main principles in order to get seats in the Government.

We do not want ministerial portfolios and posts in the Government for the sake of power or position; we do not want power for the sake of power; but we shall accept any such position only as a step towards our great objective. Between ourselves and the rest there is always the flaming sword of our world philosophy.

On the one side the State, or rather the sham State, of the Liberal-Democratic-Parliamentary stamp, forced by necessity to mask the tyranny of the financiers, and at its feet a seething mob of Jew camp-followers and place-hunters, fighting to make a living out of the system.

On our side, the fight for the liberation and purification of our people, till we achieve the true State of social justice and national liberty.

VI

CONCLUSION

What should the National Socialist know of our Programme? To answer this question was the task of this first volume of the National Socialist Library. Over and over again we have seen one truth, that runs like a red thread through all our arguments: *National Socialism is a world-philosophy which is in sharpest opposition to the modern world of Capitalism and its Marxist and bourgeois satellites.*

Our life in the service of this mighty ideal is a battle, a battle for a new Germany, and it would be no true battle if it had not a symbol, a Flag.

Can one imagine any better symbol or flag of the Commercial Party than the lamentable allegories of the '80's and '90's? Or the banners of the skittles and tobacco clubs? No! What is the flag of the Stresemann Party?

The Blacks misuse the sign of the Cross, and the Reds the old and venerable flag of the mediaeval Empire.

We National Socialists follow the fluttering battle-flag. Eternally youthful, radiant and luminous, there rises before us, on the circle of the Sun, the Hooked Cross, the symbol of reawakening life.

H

Our battle-flags, our eagles, bear this symbol.

"We are the army of the Hooked Cross.
Lift high the red flag:
We will show German labour
The road to freedom!"

APPENDIX

THE N.S.D.A.P. AND PROPERTY IN AGRICULTURAL LAND[1]

A REPLY: BY GOTTFRIED FEDER

In No. 43 of the *Deutsche Tageszeitung* (January 25, 1930) the "leading circles of the Brandenburg Landbund" put a number of questions to the N.S.D.A.P. in the name of the rural population. Their main object was to obtain a definition of the attitude of the N.S.D.A.P. towards the private ownership of land, inheritance, the raising of credits, tariffs, price regulation, profit-sharing, and questions of general social, political, and electoral interest.

I

Fearing an arbitrary interpretation of Article 17 of the N.S.D.A.P., which demands "the confiscation without indemnity of landed property illegally (!) acquired or mismanaged to the detriment of the community," they asked the following question, among other questions comprised under the first heading:

"Is the N.S.D.A.P. prepared to give guarantees that it will not encroach upon private property in land?"

Answer: National Socialism recognizes private ownership in principle, and places it under State protection. (See p. 65, II, 8.)

The healthy admixture of small, medium-sized, and large concerns will be maintained in all departments of economic life, and therefore in agriculture. (See p. 65, II, 12.)

[1] This appears in all issues up to the 475th thousand, but not in the latest German edition.

It follows, from the content and spirit of the whole Programme, clearly and irrefutably, that National Socialism, as the most convinced and consistent opponent of Marxism, most decisively repudiates its cardinal doctrine of "the confiscation of all property," a doctrine ruinous both to the nation and to its economic life, and also that National Socialism, as the keenest political adversary of the mis-guided international doctrine of Marxism, sees in a class of landowning farmers the best and surest foundation of the national State.

But being also a determined opponent of all the great capitalists whose aim it is to mobilize for themselves all agricultural values, and to oust the farmers by means of taxation and interest on loans, National Socialism expressly demands the State protection of property in land against aggression by the banks and Stock Exchanges.

We need a strong, healthy class of farmers, free from interest-slavery and taxation-Bolshevism.

II

The second question was addressed to me personally, as "having been appointed by Hitler the final arbiter of all questions touching the Programme."

"What is the attitude of National Socialism towards the inheritance of property and succession duties?"

Answer: Since it is the safeguard and mainstay of the national idea, continuity of ownership in land, i.e. the inheritance of the land which a man's forefathers reclaimed and cultivated, is a matter of course. National Socialism therefore recognizes the principle of inheritance, as it does that of private property in land.

If property goes to distant relatives the National Socialist State will levy a special tax, but in the case of closer relationship this will be assessed at the rate prevailing at the moment.

III

This question was asked owing to the quite unjustified anxiety regarding the possible consequences of the raising of loans from private capitalists on the security of the land.

Answer: A State which desires to free agricultural property from debt, and to rescue the farmers from the claws of the professional financiers—and how many farmers have already been driven from house and farm by the Jews and the Jewish banks—a State which desires to break down the financial monopoly of capitalism, and whose chief aim is to abolish the thraldom of interest, is not likely to withhold the necessary credits, nor to charge extortionate interest; on the contrary, National Socialism intends to assist agriculture to the utmost.

IV

"To abolish the thraldom of interest." To abolish unearned incomes. "What is the attitude of the National Socialist Party towards saved or inherited capital?"

Answer: What farmer has today an "unearned income" from stocks or mortgages, or what landowner can live on the interest on saved or inherited capital?

Either this question masks the anxiety of a few great landowners who still possess a little capital, or we have here an intentional misunderstanding or ignoring of this extremely important demand of the N.S.D.A.P. Programme.

N.B.—We mean literally "to abolish the *thraldom* of interest." No one will describe a few marks of interest from savings or a mortgage or Government stock as "the thraldom of interest."

But such thraldom does exist when deliberate inflation has robbed us of all our savings, and the farmer has to pay interest on fresh mortgages and short-term credits at rates which ruin him.

Those who are in favour of sticking to the present system of capitalism are opposed to the true interests of the farmers, and in favour of allowing the banks and their agents to batten on agriculture.

For the rest, I refer my readers to my pamphlets entitled *Der Staat auf nationaler und sozialer Grundlage*, and *Das Programm der N.S.D.A.P.*

V

Our policy as regards taxation is clearly and consistently stated: "To free the consumer from the burden of indirect taxation, and the producer from taxes which cramp his business."

Question: Does the Party intend to remove import duties?

Answer: The Landbund ought to be aware that the National Socialist vote in the Reichstag was absolutely in favour of protective duties on agricultural produce, in accordance with its principle—Protection of the nation's work in town and country.

VI

The question of profit-sharing arises.

It is impossible to deal here with this extremely comprehensive and difficult subject. In my weekly journal, *Die Flamme*, I have described our attitude in detail in a number of articles. Here I can only reply:

The sentences which have been removed from their context and quoted in the article in the *Deutsche Tageszeitung* are misleading. I personally consider that profit-sharing in the sense of the Capitalist and Marxist schools of ideas is not the correct solution. In this connection our Programme refers to workers in factories, and a complete elucidation of the question is not of essential importance in a pamphlet dealing with agriculture.

VII

Generous extension of Old Age Insurance Benefits:

Question: How is it proposed to raise the funds for this purpose?

Answer: There is provision now for Old Age Insurance, but it is in many cases insufficient, and is regarded as pauperization. Once the burden of tribute is removed, and those who are now unemployed but able to work are restored to the economic sphere, there will be sufficient means for providing ample old age benefits for those who are past work.

VIII, IX, X

These are questions of Party tactics, and not fundamental.

As a Party in opposition to a coalition which has brought misfortune upon Germany, we have naturally now and again to vote with the Communists (although a whole world divides us from them), just as the German National and the Christian National Farmers do. We allow no one to dictate to us as to where we obtain our adherents, but we turn to all—workers, bourgeois, and farmers—who are German at heart and are men of good will, and desire to see an end of Parliamentary misgovernment and the wretched policy of fulfilment.

We do not consider that "social intercourse" with other Parties is a proper method of freeing the German nation from Marxism and Parliamentarianism—for it usually leads to political bargaining. Nothing but dictatorial action and a ruthless will to power can pull Germany out of the morass.

The nation wants not fine words, but *force*; not bargaining, but unsparing work in the service of our poor enslaved nation.

*   *   *   *   *

Apart from these brief and condensed statements, No. 19 of the National Socialist Library—*Unser täglich Brot: Grundfragen der deutschen Landwirtschaft,* by Hermann Schneider, Eckersdorf, Kreis Namslau—gives a clear and complete account of the general attitude of National Socialism with respect to agriculture. It also contains well-conceived proposals for re-establishing the necessitous farming class of Germany.

No. 16, by Dr. Buchner, contains an excellent essay on the meaning and spirit of our economic policy.

No. 12, by Colonel Hierl, describes our policy of national defence.

We shall conclude with a few remarks as to certain questions which our political enemies spitefully misrepresent in the hope of doing us an injury.

Our attitude towards the class of permanent officials is unassailable. We should not be such fanatical admirers of the great Prussian King if we were hostile to this class. What the Army was abroad, a pure, incorruptible official class is for the State at home. Honour and duty must once again become essential qualities in our officials.

The sort of officials who are at the beck and call of the Reds and the Blacks will disappear in the coming State; there is no room for such Party bonzes in a State built upon honour and duty.

Any suggestion that the National Socialists are hostile to the officials, and intend to reduce their pay and rob them of their pensions, is simply a political lie which has been circulated by the Press of our adversaries.

On the contrary, we desire to grant to all members of the nation who have served German economy faithfully all their lives a pension of honour which will relieve them of cares in their old age. It is only thus that social assistance can be freed from the stigma of almsgiving.

We must also refer to the extension of the pension to

the independent trades and the manual workers. There is no need to worry overmuch as to how we are to raise funds for the purpose. When we cease paying thousands of millions abroad each year, and still more to our own banking houses, a fraction of those sums will suffice to pay for Old Age Pensions.

UNEMPLOYMENT ASSISTANCE AND INSURANCE

It is not, in itself, the affair of the State to support with State funds men who are able to work. If, nevertheless, we remain unshaken in our attitude towards the present system of assistance for those who cannot earn a living, if we have always pressed in Parliament for better conditions for the workless, this is not because we think it a proper state of affairs, but because a Government like the present one, whose idiotic foreign and domestic policy has swept labour, food production, and commerce in general to the edge of the abyss, is in duty bound to provide for the victims of its own policy.

A State which is unable to reinstate in the economic world millions of men who are capable of work deserves to be swept away; so that if it comes to grief over the financial problem of unemployment assistance we merely shrug our shoulders.

The various attacks on the system of the dole, even if justified when they refer to cases of abuse of this social assistance, fail to divert us from the principle in which we believe Granted that amongst nearly 3,000,000 unemployed there may be 200,000 or 300,000 notorious rogues and loafers who would soon return to work if the dole were abolished, we must not forget that there remain at least $2\frac{1}{2}$ million good workers, employees, engineers, technicians, foremen, clerks, etc., seeking desperately for work and unable to find it.

For the sake of these unhappy victims of an utterly

defective State policy the wretched principle of unemployed relief must be allowed to stand.

ATTACKS ON RELIGION AND THE CLERGY

We cannot declare too emphatically that the N.S.D.A.P. does not dream of attacking the Christian religion and its worthy servants.

But we do attack most drastically the corrupting policy of the Centre and the Bavarian People's Party; these lose no opportunity of sounding the alarm with the cry of "Religion is in Danger" except when they are making common cause with the atheistical, blasphemous Social Democrats.

It is because we have so high and holy an ideal of man's relation towards his God that we hate to see religion dragged into the dirt of political conflict.

Our attitude towards Christianity is perhaps best conveyed by the school prayers recommended by the Minister, Dr. Frick, with which I will conclude this section; it may give every Catholic and every German food for thought to hear that these prayers "are a slap in the face to every person of Catholic feelings," as the Centre Press wrote, while the Centre Minister, Dr. Wirth, wrote on May 12, 1930, to the Thuringian Ministry of State "that it affected him painfully as Minister for the Interior of the Reich when Dr. Frick recommended school prayers which contain the words: 'Lord, set us free from deceit and treason!' and 'I know that those who have neither Fatherland nor God are destroying our nation.' Such phrases cannot be harmonized with the sense and spirit of the Weimar Constitution!" (!!)

"Father, in Thy almighty hand
  Lies our nation and fatherland.
  Thou wast the strength and honour of our fathers,
  Thou art our constant weapon and defence.

Therefore set us free from deceit and treason,
Make us strong for the liberating deed,
> Give us the Saviour's heroic courage;
> Honour and liberty are the supreme good.
> Let our vow and our watchword ever be
> Germany, awake! Lord, set us free!"
>> (By an Evangelical Theologian.)

"Father in Heaven,
I believe in Thy almighty hand,
I believe in People and Fatherland,
I believe in the honour and might of our fathers,
I believe Thou art our weapon and our defence,
I believe Thou dost punish treason to our country
And dost bless the deed that frees our home.
Germany, awake to freedom!"
> (Anonymous.)

"Father in Heaven,
I believe in Thine omnipotence, justice and love,
I believe in my dear German people and fatherland.
I know that godlessness and treason to the fatherland are
   rending and destroying our people.
I know that nevertheless in our best there is the longing
   for freedom and strength to win it.
I believe that this freedom will come through the love of
   the Father in Heaven if we believe in our own
   strength."
> (By an Evangelical Schoolmaster.)

THE REQUIREMENTS OF THE PROGRAMME IN DETAIL

AS FORMULATED BY GOTTFRIED FEDER IN *DER DEUTSCHE STAAT*

THE POLICY OF THE STATE

(A) FOREIGN POLICY

1. *Creation of a closed national State, embracing all branches of the German race.*

[1]All of German blood, whether living today under French, Danish, Polish, Czech or Italian sovereignty, shall be united in a German Reich. We demand neither less nor more than what was demanded for our enemies—the right of self-determination of the Germans to belong to their motherland, to their German home.

We do not abandon a single German in Sudeten Germany, Alsace-Lorraine, Poland, the League colony of Austria, and the succession States of Austria. This demand, however, expressly excludes any tendency towards Imperialism; it is the simple and natural demand, which any powerful nationality recognizes and puts forward as a matter of course.

[2] Here is one aspect of general profit-sharing.

Why, for instance, should the great dye-works of Germany, with their predominant position of monopoly,

---

[1] This passage appeared immediately after the heading, "1. Creation of a Closed National State," etc., up to the 475th thousand of the German edition, but was omitted from the latest printing, being replaced by the three paragraphs now following the above heading.

[2] This passage concludes paragraph 23, p. 106, in all impressions up to the 475th thousand.

continue to be a mere capitalistic milch-cow for the share-holders of the I.G. Farbenindustrie, and at best—of course by raising prices—give their workers and officials "a share in the profits"?

It will be the task of the National Socialist State to see that huge monopolistic profits shall be made to serve the community by means of a very generous lowering of prices.

It is obvious that the problem is not a question of social policy, but is closely bound up with the present-day capitalistic social order (shareholder's claims).

Here we must be content with this brief statement of guiding principles; within their compass we must endeavour to introduce profit-sharing as far as possible in all businesses in which the profits go exclusively into the pockets of professional investors.

For Product Safety Concerns and Information please contact our EU
representative GPSR@taylorandfrancis.com
Taylor & Francis Verlag GmbH, Kaufingerstraße 24, 80331 München, Germany

www.ingramcontent.com/pod-product-compliance
Lightning Source LLC
Chambersburg PA
CBHW050535270326
41926CB00015B/3241